D1482273

PROUST

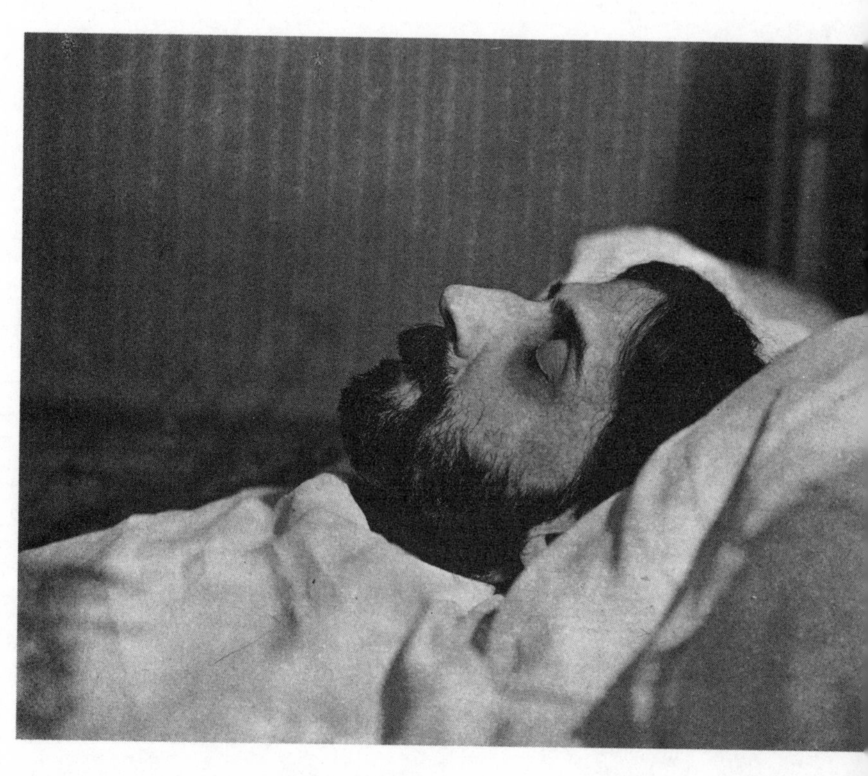

Proust

The Search

BENJAMIN TAYLOR

Yale
UNIVERSITY
PRESS

New Haven and London

Frontispiece: Man Ray, Proust on his deathbed. Man Ray Trust/Artists Rights Society (ARS), NY/ADAGP, Paris; RMN-Grand Palais/Art Resource, NY.

Yale University Press books may be purchased in quantity for educational, business, or promotional use. For information, please e-mail sales.press@yale.edu (U.S. office) or sales@yaleup.co.uk (U.K. office).

Set in Janson Oldstyle type by Integrated Publishing Solutions.
Printed in the United States of America.

Library of Congress Control Number: 2015935549
ISBN 978-0-300-16416-9 (cloth : alk. paper)

A catalogue record for this book is available from the British Library.

This paper meets the requirements of ANSI/NISO Z39.48-1992 (Permanence of Paper).

10 9 8 7 6 5 4 3 2 1

Credits appear on page 201, which constitutes a continuation of the copyright page.

IN MEMORY OF JAMES MERRILL

. . . Too violent,
I once thought, that foreshortening in Proust—
A world abruptly old, whitehaired, a reader
Looking up in puzzlement to fathom
Whether ten years or forty have gone by.
Young, I mistook it for an unconvincing
Trick of the teller. It was truth instead
Babbling through his own astonishment.

—*The Book of Ephraim*

CONTENTS

PROLOGUE

Man Ray's celebrated photo of Marcel Proust on his deathbed shows a youngish-seeming man with ringed eyes and bedclothes pulled up to his chin. Jean Cocteau had summoned Ray to 44, rue Hamelin to take the final picture. Left alone briefly with the body that afternoon, Cocteau noted the vast manuscript of *In Search of Lost Time* on the mantelpiece of the bedroom: "That pile of papers on his left was still alive, like watches ticking on the wrists of dead soldiers."[1] The date was November 18, 1922.

Death of the artist, lastingness of the work: One thinks of Proust's description in *The Captive*, the fifth volume of *In Search of Lost Time*, following the death of Bergotte, the cycle's great novelist figure, of certain bookstore windows: "The idea that Bergotte was not permanently dead is by no means improbable. They buried him, but all through that night of mourning, in the lighted shop-windows, his books, arranged three by three, kept vigil like angels with outspread wings and seemed, for him who was no more, the symbol of his resurrection."[2] As with Shakespeare, as with Balzac, as with the fictional Bergotte, fifty years and a little sufficed Marcel Proust for the completion of an ever-living imaginative universe. The million-and-a-half-word masterpiece that was, from 1909, his sole reason for living makes as large a claim on our attention as any literary work of any era. Proust's *Search* is the most encyclopedic of novels, encompassing the essentials of human nature. His cumulative breadth of understanding, in what is ostensibly a narrative of modern French life, extends to every dimension: familial, social, amatory, intellectual, artistic, religious. His account, running from the early years of the Third Republic to the aftermath of World War I, becomes the inclusive story of all lives, a colossal mimesis. To read the entire *Search* is to find oneself transfigured and victorious at journey's end, at home in time and in eternity too.

A biographer of Proust must begin with the following reversible axiom: The work is not "explained" by the life; the life is not "explained" by the work. All Proust's transactions between real life and its dramatization are in the care of the shape-shifting imagination, a creative not a recording capacity. Actual persons do not "explain" any of the characters on whom they are said to be based. Laure Hayman does not explain Odette de Crécy; Robert de Montesquiou does not explain the Baron de Charlus; neither Charles Haas nor Charles Ephrussi explains Charles Swann; Bertrand de Fenélon does not explain Robert de Saint-Loup; Albert Le Cuizat does not explain Jupien; neither the Comtesse Élisabeth Greffulhe nor the Comtesse Adhéaume de Chevigné explains Oriane de Guermantes. Still less does the historical individual named Valentin Louis Georges Eugène Marcel Proust, born to a French Jewish mother and French Catholic father in July of 1871, explain the Narrator of the *Search*. Nabokov puts the matter succinctly: Proust's book "is not a mirror of manners, not an autobiography, not a historical account."[3] The author's life, in which everything is contingent, higgledy-piggledy, disappointing, is the necessary but not sufficient precondition of an art granting deliverance, transmutation, the semblance of necessity, each thing finally in its proper place, "since the dull pain in our hearts," as Proust writes, "can raise above itself, like a banner, the visible permanence of an image."[4]

Above the dung heap of real life, art hoists its flag. That memorable metaphor occurs near the end of the *Search*, a 3,300-page epic telling of how a frightened tadpole grows up to be an omnipotent artist. Proust's book is, as Howard Moss writes, "its own self-sealing device": Our hero sits down at the end of the tale to write the book we have just finished reading.[5] A biography of Marcel Proust has a rather different, if in some ways analogous, story to tell: the coddled childhood at Paris, Auteuil, Illiers; the precocious discovery of sex; the years of schooling at Lycée Condorcet; a (surprisingly happy) year of military service in Orléans; lackadaisical university studies; his entry into the rarefied high society of the Faubourg Saint-Germain; publication of a very tentative first book, *Pleasures and Days* (1896); the consuming national drama of the Dreyfus Affair, in which Proust is active in the Captain's behalf; the grand romantic passions—for, among others, Reynaldo Hahn and Lucien Daudet; partial composition and subsequent abandonment of the autobiographical novel posthumously known as *Jean Santeuil;* Ruskin-inspired journeys to Amiens and Venice with his mother, and translations, with her assistance, of Ruskin's *The Bible of Amiens* and *Sesame and Lilies;* complex hesitation between criticism and fiction; retreat from the world and consecration to the *Search;* publication, at his own expense, of *Du côté de chez Swann* (1913); martyrizing love for Alfred Agostinelli; death of Agostinelli; outbreak of the 1914–18 War, compelling Proust to reconceive and vastly expand his book; publication of the second volume, *À l'ombre des jeunes filles en fleurs* (1918); growing fame, declining health; the struggle to finish and to correct proofs; the final emendations; the death.

At the midpoint of this life, ramifying every which way, was the Dreyfus Affair. In November 1894 a captain of the French army and Alsatian Jew named Alfred Dreyfus, falsely accused of selling military secrets to the Germans, was convicted and transported to Devil's Island to serve a life sentence. The subsequent trial and acquittal two years later of Esterhazy, the actual traitor; Zola's broadside "J'accuse . . . !"; the Captain's return from French Guiana in 1899 to stand trial a second time; his eventual exoneration in 1906—all these are strongly present in the *Search*, and at every social level. One example, from among hundreds, must suffice here: In *The Guermantes Way*, coming home from having witnessed a quarrel between Bloch, the Narrator's obnoxiously erudite Jewish friend, and M. de Norpois, a grandee of the Foreign Ministry, on the subject of Dreyfus, our hero overhears his family's butler, who is Dreyfusard, arguing with the Guermantes' butler, who is anti-Dreyfusard. Thus the Affair has riven France across all classes, as well as coining the idiom for antisemitic campaigns to come.

The Jews of the *Search* are of every moral stripe and—glory of the novel—of stripes that change. About Swann when he is dying, Proust writes in *Sodom and Gomorrah:* "Perhaps, too, in these last days, the physical type that characterizes his race was becoming more pronounced in him, alongside a sense of moral solidarity with the rest of the Jews, a solidarity which Swann seemed to have forgotten throughout his life, and which, one after another, his mortal illness, the Dreyfus case and the anti-Semitic propaganda had reawakened. There are certain Jews, men of great refinement and social delicacy, in whom nevertheless there remain in reserve and in the wings, ready to enter their lives at a given moment, as at the theater, a boor and a prophet. Swann had arrived at the age of the prophet."[6] What one can say about all of Proust's Jews is that the Affair changes their relation to what they thought they knew and held dear, and gives them the lasting sense that something atavistic has stepped into the open. Had he lived into the 1950s, Proust would have appreciated the postwar quip about going back in time to report to our pious forebears that an enlightened European people famed for philosophy, science, art, music, and poetry would one day rise up to destroy the Jews. "Those French are capable of anything," our forebears would surely have responded.

Proust's life is, like his book, a series of self-transformations; but not a series you can know from the *Search*, any more than the *Search* can be understood merely as the consequence of Proust's life. He likens the procrastinating would-be writer—which is, after all, what his hero remains for practically all of *In Search of Lost Time*—to a man who, on the morning of a duel he is unlikely to win, resolves to settle down to work if only he does not die. But he comes home unscathed only to discover he is the same as before. "As for work—exceptional circumstances having the effect of intensifying what previously existed in a man, work in the industrious, idleness in the lazy—he takes a holiday from it," not without vowing to apply himself in earnest the following day.[7] That our Narrator in the *Search* escapes, in the nick of time, a dilatoriness seemingly bred in the bone, is the novel's large-scale challenge to plausibility. But Proust's masterpiece is, as Elizabeth Bowen said, a work in which surprises small and large predominate to the last.[8] The greatest of these is that the Narrator began at all, to say nothing of finishing; that time wasted ever did get transmuted into time redeemed.

In volume two of the *Search*, *In the Shadow of Young Girls in Flower*, the preeminent painter of the age, Elstir, befriends the young Narrator at Balbec, a seaside resort on the Normandy coast. Walking the great man home one afternoon, the Narrator suddenly realizes that this master artist may once have been a certain vapid society painter, the popinjay known as Biche who used to frequent the cruel and silly circle of Mme Verdurin. He asks whether Elstir and Biche could be one and the same. "And as we were now already almost at his house, a man less distinguished of intelligence and spirit might perhaps have simply and a bit dryly bade me farewell and afterwards taken care never to see me again. But that was not how Elstir dealt with me." What the great man says to the teenager, instead of dismissing him, is one of the wisest things in Proust's Book of Wisdom, and perhaps a key with which to unlock both his life and his art: "'There is no one, however wise,' Elstir said to me, 'who has not at some time in his youth said things, or for that matter done things, which he hates to remember and would wish to have erased. But he ought not to regret them absolutely, for he could not be certain of having become wise (in the degree to which that can happen at all), unless he had gone through all the foolish or hateful forms that had led up to that last of forms. . . . The lives you admire . . . stand for fight and victory. I can see that the portrait of what we were in early days is no longer recognizable to us, and would in any event be unpleasant to look at. But it ought not to be denied, for it is a witness that we have really lived.'"[9]

Fight, victory, self-transformation. To speak biblically: the putting away of childish things. In the spring of 1891, at the age of twenty, Proust met a young man two years older than himself but already a tiger of French letters, André Gide. Proust was only a social climber with artistic pretensions, an obvious lightweight. No one who that day observed the two young men would ever have imagined that it was Proust who would come out ahead. But after the appalling waste of time, after numberless errors and follies, he retreated to his bed and green-glass lamp and wrote a Guide of the Perplexed by which we are instructed in the art of putting away, however belatedly, what we have outgrown. Who today would dream of writing a book called *How Gide Can Change Your Life?* No, it is Proust who is our contemporary.

PROUST

Chapter One

In honor of the 1867 opening of the Exposition Universelle d'Art et d'Industrie—a world's fair on the Champ de Mars intended to show off to lesser peoples Louis Napoléon's sparkling new metropole—Jacques Offenbach composed his comic opera *La Grande Duchesse de Gérolstein*, which premièred at Théâtre du Châtelet. The mighty of Europe were in attendance, including Otto von Bismarck, Prussia's Iron Chancellor, who may like others that evening have seen himself in a satiric character called Chancellor Puck, pompous leader of a joke German principality bent on war, whose General Boom, in love with the feather atop his helmet, is ready to lead the charge. Such was the note of Offenbach's *opéra bouffe.* Of all the crowned heads and dignitaries Bismarck is reported to have laughed loudest—perhaps with an eye to events three years in the future, when Prussia would annihilate the Second Empire in battle, take Louis prisoner at Sedan, besiege Paris to the point of mass starvation (dogs, cats, rats, and zoo animals were eaten), exact five billion gold francs in war reparations, confiscate Alsace and Lorraine, see King Wilhelm I of Prussia crowned emperor of a united Germany—the Second Reich—in Versailles's Hall of Mirrors, conduct a victory march up and down the Boulevard des Champs-Elysées, and return to Berlin having united Germany's principalities into a domineering nation, destroyed Europe's balance of power, and prepared the ground for vastly more destructive engagements to come.

The French Third Republic and the Paris Commune that violently resisted it were born together from Louis's defeat. Much of central Paris was burned by Communards in May 1871, the Vendôme column pulled down, the Palais Royal, Hôtel de Ville, Palais de Justice, Préfecture de Police, Louvre library and many private residences burned. The Tuileries Palace—an especially hated symbol of Napoléon III's reign that stood where now is empty ground between the two arms of the Louvre—was dynamited out of existence. Communards mined the sewers as well. Perhaps their profoundest provocation was to have set fires within Notre-Dame, put out before the cathedral could seriously catch fire.

When president Adolphe Thiers's retribution came it was savage. On May 28 his generals, Gallifet and Mac-Mahon, entered the city to finish off Communard resistance. At Père-Lachaise Cemetery the last diehards were shot against a wall sacred to this day among leftists. In the following weeks ten thousand people were executed, among them women condemned as *pétroleuses*—firebombers—and even some children. The bodies of the dead were cast into mass graves.

This insurrection and its martyrs promptly entered legend. In *The Civil War in France*, written in London as events unfolded, Karl Marx prophesied that "working-men's Paris, with its Commune, will be for ever celebrated as the glorious harbinger of a new society. Its martyrs are enshrined in the great heart of the working class."[1] (Or at least in the heart of Communist mythology: At Lenin's funeral in 1924, a faded Commune banner would drape the body.) In fewer than three months, twenty thousand Parisians had died in the fratricidal violence, more than in any previous French revolution, and Haussmann's glorious city lay mutilated. Contemplating rue de Lille on the Left Bank with its blasted houses, Théophile Gautier wrote that "it seemed to be deserted through all its length, like a street in Pompeii. . . . A silence of death reigned over these ruins; in the necropolises of Thebes or in the shafts of the Pyramids it was no more profound. No clatter of vehicles, no shouts of children, not even the song of a bird . . . an incurable sadness invaded our souls."[2] Already in June, English tourists were signing on for Cook's Tours of the burned-out rubble.

Into these circumstances Marcel Proust was born on July 10, 1871, and baptized three weeks later at the Church of Saint-Louis d'Antin.

* * *

Ten months and one week earlier, on September 3, 1870, Adrien Proust, Catholic son of a grocer in Illiers, had married Jeanne Weil, daughter of a prominent Jewish stock broker living in the wealthy eighth arrondissement of Paris at 40 *bis*, rue du Faubourg-Poissonière. Her uncle Adolphe Crémieux, a major politician of the middle decades of the nineteenth century, was among the witnesses. The marriage contract, conserved at the Bibliothèque Nationale, is marked by last-minute emendations regarding the matter of the dowry; Adrien seems to have been driving a bargain with his father-in-law-to-be. In addition to financial particulars the instrument stipulated that any children born to the union were to be baptized and brought up as Roman Catholics.

On the other hand, Jeanne herself would remain Jewish, and there is no evidence that Adrien ever pressed her to convert.

It was a marriage joining ambition to money. Having defended his thesis, "Du pneumothorax essentiel sans perforation," in 1862, Adrien had been named *chef de clinique* at the Hôpital de la Charité the following year.[3] In 1866, amid a ferocious epidemic of Asiatic cholera, he won his advanced teaching diploma and published *Differentes formes de ramolissement du cerveau.* It was cholera that would henceforth be the focus of his career. Following the lead of his teacher Pierre Charles Henri Fauvel, Adrien argued for the *cordon sanitaire* of ships entering Suez as the only way of preventing future epidemics of the disease. In the summer of 1869 Louis Napoléon's government dispatched him on an official mission to track the routes of previous choleras; he went to Astrakhan, Teheran, Mecca, Constantinople, and various cites of Egypt, returning with proposals for an effective *cordon* at Suez.

It is unknown how he and Jeanne Weil met, though one may assume at a government reception or some private social occasion. Suffice it to say that they were properly introduced, as the expression was, and had not met on a bridge or in a park. In *Jean Santeuil,* Proust's abandoned first attempt at a novel (a book that stands to *In Search of Lost Time* approximately as Joyce's *Stephen Hero* to *Ulysses*), he writes that "a marriage of love, that is to say one brought about by love, would be considered a proof of vice," whereas the union of the protagonist's parents "was not a matter of free choice, but the result of middle-class proprieties and middle-class notions of respectability; yet they will remain united until death."[4] Jeanne and Adrien spent their first night together at 8, rue Roy (near Église Saint-Augustin), where Marcel would be promptly conceived. Adrien continued his medical practice at Hôpital de la Charité throughout the Siege and the Commune, returning home on foot each evening. Jeanne, pregnant since September, was in residence at the house of her Uncle Louis Weil in nearby Auteuil, but the Siege of Paris spread hunger there too. She lost weight in the first trimester of her pregnancy. After being fired upon by a sniper in early spring Adrien also preferred Auteuil, catching the tram to and from Sainte-Sulpice station each weekday.

On May 24, 1873, twenty-two months after Marcel's birth, Jeanne was delivered of a second son, Robert, who like his brother was born at Uncle Louis's house in Auteuil. Though the Prousts surely paid scant attention that day to political events, May 24 was momentous for the young Third Republic: Adolph Thiers, devoutly republican, resigned as president, succeeded by Patrice de Mac-Mahon, Duc de Magenta, devoutly royalist. With the Comte de Chambord, grandson of Charles X and Legitimist claimant to the title king of France—in waiting at Frohsdorf Castle near Vienna, addressed as "Majesté," and styled Henri V by his followers—a Bourbon restoration seemed in the offing. Indeed Chambord would have been crowned but for his unwillingness to accept the tricolor as France's flag. It was to be the old *drapeau blanc fleurdelisé* or nothing; thus perished French royalist hopes.

The Prousts moved that summer from rue Roy to more spacious quarters at nearby 9, boulevard Malesherbes, the six-room, second-story apartment where they would live for the next twenty-seven years. Weekends were typically at Uncle Louis's, where one of the two gatehouses was always ready to receive them. (A merry widower, Uncle Louis had numerous mistresses, including the renowned cocotte Laure Hayman—subsequently shared, it seems, with Dr. Proust.) Easter holidays and summers were at the house of Uncle Jules and Aunt Élisabeth Amiot at Illiers, 5, rue du Saint-Esprit (now known to the world as Tante Léonie's House in Illiers-Combray). These two pastorals, Illiers and Auteuil, were to blend into the Combray of the *Search*. As Proust's great French biographer Jean-Yves Tadié says: "Auteuil belonged to his maternal lineage, Illiers was his paternal heritage. They would both be fused, through

5, Rue du Saint-Esprit, Illiers. Nicolas Drogoul

memory, into a blessed unity which makes it impossible to distinguish any longer between two branches of the same tree."[5]

Regarding Jeanne as his own daughter, Uncle Louis in 1876 added a wing for her and her family. Twenty-four years later, following his death, Uncle Louis's house at Auteuil would be sold. The new owner razed it in 1901 to make way for a block of flats (pulled down in their turn to make way for a new thoroughfare, avenue Mozart). Among the most affecting moments in *Jean Santeuil* is the mother's grief over that vanished house: "Monsieur and Mme Santeuil had changed a good deal since the day when we saw them for the first time in the little garden in Auteuil, on the ruins of which there rose three or four six-story houses, several of which had already been let." Whenever they pass by "what for her was the saddest of tombs," Monsieur Santeuil says to his wife, "Close your eyes." And in the opening movement of the *Search* our prematurely old Narrator recollects this lost paradise—the only true kind, he will later say—in which he stood frozen on the staircase, longing for Maman's goodnight kiss and terrified of his father's anger: "Many years have passed since that night. The wall of the staircase up which I had watched the light of his candle gradually climb was long ago demolished. And in myself, too, many things have perished which I imagined would last forever."[6] Thus the centrifuge of imagination combines the demolished mansion at Auteuil with the still-standing Illiers house of Aunt Élisabeth and Uncle Jules Amiot in order to produce a place existing only on the charmed map of literature: Aunt Léonie's Combray house.

Though Jeanne's diaries have disappeared, one can assemble from letters an image of the upper-middle-class daughter and wife, superior of her kind. High intelligence and flying wit were the traits, alongside an unaffected learning possessed without benefit of the *baccalauréat* or, it seems, any schooling away from home. She was a worldly Jewish girl on the easiest terms with the civilization that had enfranchised her German-born grandparents. Still very much a Weil after marriage, she saw her parents and brother Georges nearly every day. The attachment to her mother, Adèle—"more Sevigné than Sevigné herself," Jeanne said—was exceptional. As Marcel described it, when Grand'mère would rise to leave, Maman would accompany her as far as the drawing-room door, where they would broach new topics. After slowly descending to the foyer, still talking, they would sit down at the door to the courtyard and talk for another half-hour, after which Grand'mère would take note of the time and walk her daughter back upstairs. (A family style known with few variations across a range of cultures: goodbye without leaving.)

Jeanne took evident pride in Adrien, acknowledged throughout Europe as a leading man in his field. Author in 1875 of *An Essay on International Hygiene*, four years later he ascended to the Académie de médecine. On the subject of her country in-laws back in Illiers she was notably close-mouthed. Not her sort, one may safely assume, nor was she theirs. The polyglot, musical, artistic, and literary product of high Parisian *juiverie* had little curiosity about the modest clan she'd married into. At Illiers her reflections on Mme de Sévigné and Berlioz cannot have drawn much return fire. Still and all it was the name of Proust, not that of Weil, that was anciently French, recorded in the little town's annals as far back as 1589.

In 1880 Jeanne grieved a pair of deaths: her great uncle Adolphe Crémieux's, followed quickly by that of his wife, Amélie *née* Berncastel, elder sister of Jeanne's maternal grandmother. As minister of justice, Crémieux had in 1848 done away with the death penalty for political crimes and abolished slavery in the colonies. Aunt Amélie was remarkable in her own right as one of the leading literary *salonnières* of the Romantic period: Lamartine, Hugo, Musset, Mérimée, and Dumas were among her familiars. Such was the atmosphere that Jeanne's mother imbibed in lieu of formal education. Uncle Adolphe was in effect her private tutor; Aunt Amélie had introduced her niece Adèle, Marcel's grandmother, to the literary firmament. It was a cosmopolitan angle on life—distinctively Bercastelian, Weilian—that she would pass on to Jeanne, who passed it in turn to Marcel.

* * *

On a family outing to the Bois de Boulogne one pollen-filled afternoon in the spring of 1881, nine-year-old Marcel suffered his first attack of asthma, the disease that would dominate his life and eventually kill him. Long years later his brother Robert recalled that spring day, Marcel struck by a frightening spasm of suffocation that, while the terrified family watched, might well have been fatal. Proust himself broached the topic of his attacks only once in the published works—in "The Indifferent One," an early story he chose never to reprint after its magazine appearance: "A child who from birth has been able to breathe without thinking about it does not know how essential to life is the air, which he is not even aware of, that fills his breast so sweetly. Has he, in a bout of fever, or a convulsion just been suffocating? In the desperate efforts he makes, he is struggling, with his entire being, for his life, for his lost tranquility, which can only be restored to him with the air from which he never knew he could be separated."[7]

Across the Seine, in the rue des Ursulines, steps from the Jardin du Luxembourg, was Marcel's first school, his *école maternelle*, the Cours Pape-Carpentier. There he came under the spell of a handsome boy, Jacques Bizet, son of Geneviève Halévy Bizet and the renowned composer Georges Bizet, dead of a heart attack at thirty-seven following the failure of his opera *Carmen*. (Visitors to the Musée d'Orsay will have seen Jules-Élie Delaunay's striking 1878 portrait of Mme Bizet in mourning.) Both mother and son would be consequential in Marcel's life. Jacques followed Marcel in the autumn of 1882 to *cinqième* (eighth grade) at lycée Fontannes, shortly to be renamed lycée Condorcet, a five-minute walk from the Prousts' apartment on boulevard Malesherbes.

This extraordinary school, the most literary of the *grandes lycées*, nourished Marcel in ways the sterner establishments across the river, Saint-Louis, Henri IV, or Louis-le-Grand, probably could not have done. If the great writers can be divided into school haters and school lovers, Proust certainly belongs to the latter category, owing to the invigorating curriculum and distinguished staff of "the light and charming Condorcet,"[8] as Marcel's classmate Robert Dreyfus would recall it, which boasted among its alumni Jules and Edmond de Goncourt, Charles Augustin Sainte-Beuve, Théodore de Banville, Paul Verlaine, Hippolyte Taine, and Henri Bergson, as well as the great physicist and mathematician André-Marie Ampère and three presidents of the Third Republic. (In days to come, Jean Cocteau would also study there.) The school's atmosphere is ecstatically remembered by another classmate, Fernand Gregh, in his 1947 memoir *Age of Gold:* "To try to enumerate the beauties disclosed one by one to us in those days would be an impossible task. Suffice it to say we were young and the world was alight with our continual poetry."[9]

A number of Marcel's Condorcet essays are conserved at the Bibliothèque Nationale. In one from *quatrième* (ninth grade), intended as a pastiche of Plutarch, he writes: "The study of literature enables us to scorn death; it raises us above earthly matters by speaking to us of the things of the mind; it refines our spirit, a rational, almost philosophical courage much finer than physical courage or the vigor of the senses for it is in reality the valor of the spirit."[10] Strip this of its youthful bravado and you have a rudimentary version of the wisdom of *In Search of Lost Time:* that there is a way past life's forfeitures, a way to timelessness. But no more for the aging man than the growing boy would God have a part in these inklings. At the church of Saint-Louis-Antin, in autumn 1883, he took his first and last communion. There is no trace of any religious practice beyond this date.

Prior to Marcel's tenth-grade year, with its demanding curriculum of Greek, Latin, French literature, German, Roman history and natural sciences, the Prousts took an August holiday at Houlgate on the Normandy coast. Nearly forty years later, at Marcel's funeral, an old man whose name does not survive approached the famous art dealer and friend of Proust René Gimpel and said he'd been little Marcel's Greek tutor that long-ago Houlgate summer; that the boy had in those days been drunk with a longing for the theater: "Do you think one day my plays will be performed at the Comédie-Française?" he had asked the tutor and his wife.[11]

In the event, Marcel was absent from *troisième* more than present. At puberty his asthma led to frequent bronchitis and general bad health. The next year, *seconde* or eleventh grade, was still worse; he was forced to repeat it the following year. It was probably at the age of fourteen, during that abortive first try at *seconde*, that he made the boyish discovery he would one day describe better than any writer before him. In *Swann's Way* the hero tells of his frightened bliss "when, at the top of our house at Combray, in the little room that smelt of orris-root, . . . with the heroic misgivings of a traveler setting out on a voyage of exploration or of a desperate wretch hesitating on the verge of self-destruction, faint with emotion, I explored across the bounds of my own experience, an untrodden path which for all I knew was deadly—until the moment when a natural trail like that left by a snail smeared the leaves of the flowering currant that drooped around me."[12] But a still more explicit version survives in *Contre Sainte-Beuve:* "At last, an opalescent jet squirted from me in successive bursts, each one like the moment when the fountain at Saint-Cloud leaps up."[13]

If these were sickly years they were also a time of extraordinary ferment. He wrote "The Eclipse," his first story. At the request of Antoinette Faure, a childhood playmate from the Champs-Élysées and daughter of Félix Faure, future president of France, he answered a series of questions in an English keepsake book: "*Your favourite qualities in a man.*"—"Intelligence, moral sense." "*Your favourite qualities in a woman.*"—"Tenderness, naturalness, intelligence." "*Your idea of misery.*"—"To be separated from Maman." "*Where would you like to live?*"—"In the realm of the ideal, or rather of my ideal." "*Your favourite heroines in real life.*"—"A woman of genius leading the life of an ordinary woman." "*For what fault have you the most toleration?*"—"For the private lives of geniuses."[14] Age fifteen proved a crucial year of reading. On his last holiday at Illiers (Adrien would conclude that the country air was exacerbating the boy's asthma and put the Beauce region out of bounds), he tore through Augustin Thierry's *History of the Norman Conquest.* At Salies-de-Béarn, near Biarritz, with his mother and Robert, he read Alphonse Daudet's *Tartarin of Tarrascon.* More ambitiously, he tackled Tolstoy's *Anna Karenina*, George Eliot's *Middlemarch*, and *The*

Mill on the Floss, numerous titles by Robert Louis Stevenson, Galland's version of *The Arabian Nights*, and Dostoyevsky's *The Idiot* (which he would come to regard as the greatest of all novels). Large swaths of Balzac's *Comédie Humaine* were consumed. Indeed much of the literature that would be most important to Proust was internalized during this period of insatiable reading. In the following two years, the Parnassian Leconte de Lisle replaced Alfred de Musset as his favorite poet. Gérard de Nerval's *Sylvie* he proclaimed the most moving story ever written. *The Life of Jesus*, by Ernest Renan, a family friend, solidified his irreligious predisposition. Among contemporary French novelists he favored Pierre Loti and Anatole France, two of the best. But like the rest of his generation, he fell for the silver-tongued sub-Romanticism of Maurice Barrès's *The Cult of the Self.*

The publishing sensation of 1886 had been a book Marcel did not read, though could scarcely have remained unaware of. Édouard Drumont, founder in 1869 of the Anti-Semitic League of France, who six years later would establish *La Libre parole*, the leading French antisemitic newspaper, published *La France Juive* (Jewish France), which sold 100,000 copies in two months and became the sacred text of French Jew-hatred. The boy no doubt felt that this squalor had no bearing on him; between asthma attacks, his existence was indeed pleasant. In 1887 he sat for a studio portrait by Paul Nadar, the preeminent social photographer of Paris. In it Marcel is still a child, an awkward-looking one at that, with a too-long nose. Still, the shorn head is high, the collar stiffly correct, the tie in foulard style. While the cheeks retain their baby fat, on his upper lip is a darkening of down. In a gesture at manhood he wears a watch chain across the double-breasted jacket: a youth not yet in flower but who, once adolescence is done, will know what it is to be beautiful.

He played at love with Marie Benardaky, daughter of a rich

Russian merchant who in younger days had been master of ceremonies at the court of Tsar Alexander II. Here, from *Jean Santeuil*, is an intimation of what he felt: "All the time she was present, he stayed close behind her, taking part in games of prisoner's base, hide-and-seek and sliding. When she arrived at about three in the Champs-Elysées with her governess and her sister, his heart beat so fast that he almost fell down."[15]

So much for make-believe. The real erotics were at Condorcet. To Jacques Bizet he wrote: "I always find it sad not to pluck the delicious flower that soon enough we'll no longer be able to pick. For it will then be fruit . . . forbidden."[16] And to Jacques's even handsomer cousin, Daniel Halévy: "I've got friends of great intelligence and moral refinement who, I daresay, have on occasion enjoyed themselves with a friend. . . . That was in the prime of youth. Later on, they went back to women. Don't think of me as a pederast. That would hurt. Morally speaking, I make every effort, if only by dint of elegance, to keep myself pure."[17] As if in atonement for such frankness, he passed the following unfavorable verdict on himself in a letter to Robert Dreyfus, another of their Condorcet set: "I must confess I don't like him"—Marcel Proust—"much, with his perpetual over-enthusiasms, his fussy ways, his tremendous passions and his adjectives."[18]

Both parents were concerned about their elder son's inclinations and, in particular, about an obvious passion for Jacques. In the spring of 1888 Adrien caught Marcel masturbating and gave him ten francs to go to a whorehouse. That an epidemiologist father, in an era of rampant venereal disease, would have done this seems strange, not to say deplorable, though he needn't have worried. Marcel disgraced himself by failing to perform and added insult to injury when he broke the prostitute's chamber pot. I hazard that no reader of this biography has written a letter to his grandfather such as the one Marcel wrote the following day to Nathé Weil: "I needed to see a woman so badly in order to cure my bad habit of masturbation that Papa gave me 10 francs to go to the brothel, but first in my turmoil I broke a chamber pot, 3 francs, second in all this same turmoil I was unable to fuck. So there I was, just as I was before needing 10 francs more to release myself and these further 3 francs for the pot. But I dare not ask Papa for money so soon and I was hoping that you would come to my aid in circumstances which as you know are not only exceptional but, let's face it, *unique*."[19]

* * *

That summer Marcel began private philosophical tutorials with a family friend and *Revue bleue* contributor, Paul Desjardins, whose name would one day crop up in *Swann's Way*. (The insufferable Legrandin, who masks snobbery with flowery talk and a pretense of unworldliness, quotes a line from Desjardins.) Together they read Heraclitus and Lucretius. Desjardins's much later description of his pupil is among the best we have from this period: "The young Persian prince with huge gazelle eyes and languorous eyelids; an expression at once respectful, undulating, caressing, and anxious; a collector of pleasures for whom nothing was dull; irritated by the obstacles with which nature thwarted man's efforts—especially so fragile a man as he; endeavoring to make something out of the passivity that seemed to be his lot; who strove for the *most*, for what was *too much*, even in his delightful kindness: this romantic child, I draw readily from memory."[20] A great hater of fashionable society, Desjardins would drop Marcel once he observed the youngster's growing fascination with aristocratic personalities of the Faubourg Saint-Germain.

In October at Condorcet Marcel began studying with a brilliant and charismatic professor of philosophy, Alphonse Darlu, to whom on the shortest acquaintance he unburdened himself in a letter of uncanny psychological sophistication: "When I read a poem by Leconte de Lisle, for instance, all the time that I am enjoying the infinite sensual delights as I did in the past, the other *I* is watching me, enjoying observing the causes of my pleasure, seeing a certain connection in them between myself and the work, and thus destroying the certainty of the work's own beauty. Above all it immediately starts imagining different prerequisites for beauty, and finally kills all my enjoyment."[21] Here he touches on the specter that would haunt him in his long, awkward, and mistake-ridden path to originality: a debilitating self-consciousness. As with the hero of *In Search of Lost Time*, vitality seems checkmated by the excess of self-seeing, a curse to be lifted only in the final sequence of *Time Regained* when a self-forgetful confidence carries all before it.

Alphonse Darlu appears as M. Beulier in *Jean Santeuil*, and Proust always insisted on him as the man most influential to his thinking. After Proust's death members of the Darlu family recollected how the young disciple would accompany the weary professor home and detain him on the doorstep with Socratic conversation.[22]

These years of *rhétorique*, the last stage of *lycée* training, were a vibrant time, in the classroom and out. Marcel worked successively on two school magazines, the *Revue verte* and the *Revue lilas*. (No copies of either survive.) He became an avid operagoer, attending *Cendrillion*, *Atalie*, *Mimi*, *Amante du Christ*, and *Mignon* in a single season. Sometime in the autumn of 1888 at Auteuil he met Laure Hayman, former lover of Uncle Louis Weil and (very likely, as I have said) of Dr. Proust as well. Her current lover was the popular novelist Paul Bourget; Laure had provided the model for his most recent heroine, *Gladys Harvey*. This was Marcel's first acquaintance with a *grande cocotte*. In the fullness of time she would serve him as one model for Odette de Crécy, whom we meet first as Uncle Louis's "lady in pink," then as Swann's adored mistress, and later still as his unloved wife. (Laure Hayman, unlike the cunning but stupid Odette, was a *femme d'esprit* with genuine talent. Proust's characters always diverge from their putative models.)

Most important, Marcel began to attend the sumptuous Saturdays of Jacques Bizet's mother—now Geneviève Straus—at 134, boulevard Haussmann. Remarried, she had emerged as one of the most renowned *salonnières* of the day. ("I was the first to know and to love you," she would write to Proust in the last months of his life.)[23] At her apartment Marcel met the likes of Edgar Degas, Gabriel Fauré, Sarah Bernhardt, Guy du Maupassant, Charles Haas (sole Jewish member of the hyperexclusive Jockey Club), Princess Mathilde Bonaparte, and others of the new and old nobility. Paintings by Claude Monet and Gustave Moreau adorned the walls. Years later, Gustave Schlumberger, the historian of Byzantium, was to write: "On a stool at the feet of Madame Geneviève Straus one constantly saw the bizarre Marcel Proust, still a young man, who since then has written books admired by some and incomprehensible to others, including myself."[24]

This was the first stage of Marcel's long march through the fashionable world, a preparation of great importance and also—as for any gifted young person—a beguilement and a danger. Of these transient excitements he would write in volume two of *In Search of Lost Time*, *In the Shadow of Young Girls in Flower*: "One becomes a different man, every drawing room being a fresh universe in which, coming under the sway of a new moral perspective, we fasten our attention, as if they were to matter to us for all time, on people, dances, card-tables, all of which we shall have forgotten by the morning."[25]

In the autumn, Marcel made another attempt to win the heart of Daniel Halévy, sending him a poem entitled "Pederasty": "I want to bed, to love, to live forever / With a warm child, Jacques, Pierre, or Firmin," only to backpedal afterward. He had formed the habit of confessing his homosexual desires, then denying them, as correspondence with Daniel subsequent to the poem reveals. This pattern of admitting and retracting was to last for the rest of Proust's life.

* * *

Two ways in the world, two goals, beckoned to the favored youth. One was love—in other words, homosexual longing. The other was the *beau monde*—in other words, social climbing. Besides Mme Straus's *salon* Marcel also frequented, at Trouville on the Normandy coast, that of Mme Arthur Baignères at her beautiful house Les Frémonts—immortalized in the *Search* as "La Raspelière." Upon graduation from Condorcet—*bachelier ès lettres*, third in the class and winner of first prize for French composition —Marcel took his summer holiday (the first ever not in the company of parents) in 1889 at Ostende, in Flemish Belgium, with a school friend, Horace Finaly, whose lively family he promptly fell in love with and idealized. These were Jews far grander than the Weils. Horace's father, Hugo Finaly, chief of the Banque de Paris et des Pays Bas, would be the model for Sir Rufus Israels in the *Search*. Falling in love with a tribe who seem preferable to one's own—it would happen more than once to young Marcel.

Connections begat connections. There were further *salons* to conquer. Upon his return to Paris, Marcel was introduced by his old classmate Fernand Gregh to a leading writer of the day, Anatole France, at 12, avenue Hoche, home of Léontine Arman de Caillevet *née* Lippmann, the novelist's married mistress, whose faithful nucleus included Leconte de Lisle, Renan, Clemenceau, Charles Maurras, Dumas *fils*, Heredia, Poincaré, Jean Jaurès, Maurice Barrès, and other notables from politics and letters, a spectrum encompassing socialists and right-wing xenophobes and all shades between. Interestingly, these afternoons were devoid of music or musicians, for Mme Arman, like her lover Anatole France, loathed music. This Arman milieu is evoked in Gregh's *Age of Gold:* "Quite impossible to praise adequately the flying ripostes, refinements of humor, dextrous delivery, startling epigrams."[26]

As well, from this season, there is Colette's astringent depiction of Marcel in *Claudine en ménage* (1902): "One Wednesday, at the house of Ma Barmann [Mme Arman], I was cruised by a young pretty-boy of letters. (Beautiful eyes, that kid, a touch of conjunctivitis, but never mind . . .) He compared me to Myrtocleia, to a young Hermes, to a cupid by Prud'hon; he ransacked his memory and secret museums for me, quoting so many hermaphrodite masterpieces that . . . he almost spoiled my enjoyment of a divine cassoulet, the specialty of the house. . . . My little flatterer, excited by his own evocations, didn't let go of me. . . . Nestled in my Louis XV basket chair, I heard him, without really listening, parade his literary knowledge." (Colette in fact wrote "young kike [*youpin*] of letters," which "Willy," the lazy fraud of a husband for whom she ghostwrote the Claudine series, emended to "pretty boy.)"[27]

Eighteen eighty-nine, the year of all this climbing, was also the year in which the Prousts' friend Gustave Eiffel was under fire for having modified the Parisian skyline, his colossal tower now dominating the world's fair with which republican France marked the centenary of its Revolution. It was also the year in which a revanchist and monarchist adventurer, General Georges Boulanger, threatened to topple the Republic before fleeing to Brussels to kill himself at the grave of a mistress he'd lost the previous year. Boulangism was a deeply bizarre episode, exposing extremist elements that would coalesce again a decade later in the persecution of Captain Alfred Dreyfus. An unpolitical young man in 1889, eighteen and on frolics of his own, Marcel paid scant attention to the Boulangist melodrama. But ten years later, when Captain Dreyfus's retrial at Rennes riveted the world's attention and caused the Third Republic to totter, he would follow events as passionately as anyone in France.

Chapter Two

On July 15, 1889, the Chambre des Deputés passed a new law requiring every eighteen-year-old Frenchman to serve one year in the military. Eighteen eighty-nine was the only year in which enrollees were allowed to choose where they wished to train. Realizing this, Marcel enlisted ahead of his call-up as a soldier second-class, commencing in November twelve months of military service at Orléans, the place of his choice, in the 76th Infantry Regiment, 1st Batallion, 2nd Company, billeted in the Coligny barracks. In a passage from "Tableaux de genre de souvenir," a brief memoir of the military year, he was to praise "the rural character of the places, the simplicity of some of my peasant comrades whose bodies were more beautiful and more agile, their minds more original, their hearts more spontaneous, their characters more natural than in the case of the young men I had known before, or those I knew afterwards."[1]

Add to this that his immediate commanding officer was

Comte Armand-Pierre de Cholet, a dashing swell of the Faubourg, as much at home at the Jockey Club or the Cercle de la Rue Royale as in barracks. Equally winning was the company captain, Comte Charles Colonna-Walewski, who wore lightly the distinction of being Napoléon I's grandson through the emperor's dalliance in Poland with Maria Walewska. In the *Search* the Narrator visits his great friend Robert de Saint-Loup, garrisoned at Doncières, an Orléans-like town where the cavalry captain is one Prince Borodino, in whose face and gestures everyone detects Napoléon the Great, his grandfather. But the Narrator notes in him as well—here fiction going the facts one better—certain mannerisms of Napoléon III, his unacknowledged but likely father: "It was with the sharpness of the first Emperor in his voice that he addressed a reprimand to a corporal, with the dreamy melancholy of the second that he exhaled a puff of cigarette-smoke."[2] In the *Search* Prince Borodino consents to have the Narrator, a civilian, sleep in barracks during his stay. In real life, soldier Proust's presence there developed into a serious problem. His nightlong attacks of asthma were severe enough to keep the other men from sleeping. Marcel was ordered to take rooms in town at the boardinghouse of Mme Ronvoyzé in rue du Faubourg Bannier. (A faithfully autobiographical version of this is to be found in *Jean Santeuil.*)

Each Sunday of his military year Marcel would journey from Orléans to Auteuil to be with Jeanne and the family. Adèle Weil's health had declined and beginning in mid-December she was acutely ill of uremia. On January 3, 1890, one month short of her sixty-sixth birthday, Grand'mère died. It was Marcel's first experience of death, and he was helpless in the face of his mother's wild grief. After the prescribed months of *deuil*—first black wool, then black silk—she refused to go on to the gray or dark colors, continuing in full mourning to the end of her life.

* * *

Proust's *In Search of Lost Time* will be a vast sorting out, a moral accounting as comprehensive as Dante's in *The Divine Comedy.* The whole moral scale is present, from Charlie Morel—who is, among other things, a rapist—to the only character in those pages who is without sin and an absolute: Batilde, the Narrator's grandmother. In *Axel's Castle* Edmund Wilson calls her the moral equivalent of the speed of light: nothing beyond Grand'mère, nothing to compare to her. Our hero must journey, like the rest of us, from selfishness to selfishness, vanity to vanity, delusion to delusion. But one cannot imagine Grand'mère having been selfish, vain, or deluded at any age. She is love, she is naturalness, she is unfallenness. When she goes, a radiance is snatched from the world. Nothing is ever the same again.

Death, likened to a sculptor, first sets his chisel upon her in the Champs-Élysées. While her grandson waits in bored irritation, longing to join friends, Grand'mère enters a public toilet and suffers a stroke. Thirty minutes pass, long enough for the lavatory attendant, known as "La Marquise," to report to the boy on the bowel habits of other customers, about whom she is brutally snobbish. An ill-dressed woman, though frantic to relieve herself, is turned away. "Looked like a bad payer," the "Marquise" snorts. There is Shakespearean bravura in this joining of the low and homely to the tragic. When Grand'mère finally reappears, "I looked at her more closely," says the Narrator, "and was struck by the disjointedness of her gait. Her hat was crooked, her cloak stained; she had the disheveled and disgruntled appearance, the flushed, slightly dazed look of a person who has just been knocked down by a carriage or pulled out of a ditch." To hide from her grandson what has happened, she tries to avert her face.

Thus her dying begins; then gallops. The doctor orders an injection of morphine and cylinders of oxygen. "My mother, the doctor, the nursing sister held these in their hands; as soon as one was exhausted another was put in its place. I had left the room for a few minutes. When I returned I found myself in the presence of a sort of miracle. Accompanied by an incessant low murmur, my grandmother seemed to be singing us a long, joyous song which filled the room, rapid and musical." But for the morphine and oxygen cylinders, it could be a death watch in any century. "When my lips touched her face, my grandmother's hands quivered, and a long shudder ran through her whole body—a reflex, perhaps, or perhaps it is that certain forms of tenderness have, so to speak, a hyperaesthesia which recognizes through the veil of unconsciousness what they scarcely need senses to enable them to love."[3]

But none of this is in fact Proust's memory of the death of his own grandmother in 1890. The scene from *The Guermantes Way*, among the most famous in French literature, immortalizes an experience that would befall Marcel only fifteen years later, when the death of Jeanne all but destroyed him. *In Search of Lost Time* takes the form of an autobiography, but not Marcel Proust's. It is the redemptive tale of a wayfarer whose Christian name may be Marcel but whose surname is undivulged, astray along the Guermantes way and the way past Swann's place, and who must know to the full every disillusionment each has to offer. "Was it the same with all one's social relations?" asks the Narrator in *The Guermantes Way*. "And into what depths of despair might this not someday plunge me, if it were to be the same with love? That was the future's secret."[4]

* * *

He met at Orléans a young gunner from 30th Artillery Regiment, Robert de Billy, Protestant and cosmopolitan, who would be Marcel's lifelong friend, different though they were, as different, Billy would later say, as Flaubert's Bouvard and Pécuchet. Billy was destined for a distinguished diplomatic career; among his postings were Rome, where he was first secretary, and much later Tokyo, where in the twenties he succeeded Paul Claudel as ambassador. Cherishing the memory of Marcel throughout his long life, Billy said their friendship had taught him the pleasure of evading categories or abstractions—"*la joie de penser autrement que par principes.*"[5] Can there be a better definition of artistic thinking?

At Orléans there would be no repeating the honors and distinctions of Condorcet: Marcel placed sixty-third out of sixty-four in the military examination. He seems to have been indulged because of obvious bad health. But indulgence went only so far. Attempting to reenlist at the conclusion of his military year, he was declared unsuitable, though he did remain on the roster as a *sous-officier* in the reserve. Mustered out, he enrolled, at his parents' urging, in the Faculté de droit and the École libre des sciences politiques in order to pursue degrees simultaneously in government and law—not uncommon at the time, though Marcel had left behind the habit of classroom application, dreamed of more glamorous purlieus, and made a very feeble graduate student.

In addition to the *salons* of Mme. Straus and Mme. Lemaire, Proust made his way into that of Mme Arman de Caillavet, where he was befriended by Gaston Arman, her son, later a successful dramatist, and met Jeanne Pouquet, with whom Gaston was in love. In a gesture of chivalric playacting that would be characteristic, Marcel paid court to her, whom he would later call the second great love of his life after little Marie Benardaky. This tendency is familiar to most young homosexuals obliged to dissimulate what they feel: displacement of romantic love for a friend onto the friend's sweetheart. An antic photo taken at the rue Bineau tennis court shows a kneeling Marcel, who strums the strings of a tennis racquet as if it were a mandolin. This mock serenade tells the whole story: Marcel's attentions to the opposite sex remained chastely gallant for the simple reason that they were passionless. As for Gaston, he seems to have understood that there was no cause for alarm.

That was the summer of 1891 and Proust, now twenty, was taking his first literary steps. In February, *Le Mensuel* had included a poem of his called simply "Poetry," along with "During Lent," a review-essay about the leading cabaret singer of the day, Yvette Guilbert. In May, at Gabriel Trarieux's apartment, the unprofitable meeting with Gide took place. (The next connection between them was to be twenty years later when, at Nouvelle Revue Française, after sampling only two sentences, Gide rejected the manuscript of *Swann's Way* as unpublishable.)[6] In the October number of *Le Mensuel* two more works saw the light: an unsigned short story, "Memory," and a piece of landscape writing, "Norman Things," in which the glimmers of something distinctively Proustian are present: "And so this countryside, the richest in France—which with its limitless abundance of farms, cattle, cream, cider-apple trees and thick lawns summons us only to eat and sleep—adorns itself with a certain mystery once night has fallen and vies in melancholy with the vast plain of the sea."[7]

He'd written this while on holiday in Cabourg at the summer retreat of Mme Arthur Baignères. There he encountered Jacques-Émile Blanche, who sketched him one evening. A lifelong friendship—though not an easy one—began between artist and writer. It was Blanche who made the introduction to Oscar Wilde at Mme Baignères's Paris house, where Marcel peppered him with questions about English literature and invited him to dine at boulevard Malesherbes, evidently eliding from the invitation that he lived with his parents and that they would be present. To make matters worse, on the evening of this ill-fated dinner Marcel had yet to return home when Wilde presented himself. The celebrated Irishman gazed around, then said to Dr. and Mme Proust, "How ugly your house is!"—an insult Proust was to put into the mouth of the Baron de Charlus in *The Captive*—and retreated to the lavatory. Upon Marcel's tardy arrival Wilde emerged to say he had imagined they would be dining alone, then took his leave.

Thirty years later, in Proust's extraordinary prelude to *Sodom and Gomorrah*, it is a disgraced and imprisoned Wilde we meet among the accursed race of inverts: "Their honour precarious, their liberty provisional, lasting only until the discovery of their crime; their position unstable, like that of the poet one day fêted in every drawing room and applauded in every theatre in London, and the next driven from every lodging, unable to find a pillow on which to lay his head, turning the mill like Samson."[8]

* * *

At the start of 1892 Fernand Gregh, along with a few other Condorcet alumni, founded a new literary review, *Le Banquet*, which would last from March of that year to March of the following. July's issue featured three "études" by Proust, one of them including the following sentence: "Desire makes all things flourish, possession withers them." And in a review he wrote: "The day comes when we understand that tomorrow can be no different than yesterday since yesterday is what tomorrow is composed of." Intimations of themes unborn.[9]

It is also in 1892 that Marcel, in this phase both a student and a practitioner of snobbery, is received by his "first royal," as the Narrator would say ("ma première altesse"), albeit of the Napoleonic kind. This was Princess Mathilde, daughter of Jérôme Bonaparte, niece of Napoléon I, cousin of Napoléon III, who included the young contributor to *Le Banquet* in her evenings at 20, rue de Courcelles. A lively, disarming woman ("If it weren't for the French Revolution, I would be selling oranges in the streets of Ajaccio!"), the princess counted among her renowned adherents Edmond de Goncourt (who would mock her cruelly in his *Journal*), Gustave Schlumberger, José-Maria de Heredia, and Georges de Porto-Riche. Still more important were the noble dead of her *salon:* in their day, Flaubert, Dumas *père*, Merimée, and Sainte-Beuve had all been familiars. Jolly or strict as the occasion warranted, Princess Mathilde had famously dismissed Hippolyte Taine with a calling card marked P.P.C.—*pour prendre congé* (by way of taking leave)—on account of some slight to the Sanctified Uncle's memory.

At her house Marcel met Charles Ephrussi, art authority and man about town, whose Jewish grandfather had cornered the wheat market in Odessa and founded a dynasty first at Constantinople, then in Vienna and Paris. (It was Charles who, in 1871, purchased the netsuke collection written about so beautifully by his descendant Edmund de Waal in *The Hare with Amber Eyes.*) Charles moved with ease in all the best *salons* and was counted an intimate in particular of Princess Matilde's establishment, notable for its absence of antisemitism. Proust's lifelong friend Léon Daudet wrote in his diary after an evening there: "The imperial dwelling was infested with Jews and Jewesses."[10] Orientally rich, ambitiously self-invented, socially omnipresent, Charles was exactly the sort of figure to make a target for such people and would earn the particular loathing of Goncourt.

But where Goncourt and young Daudet saw only an *arriviste*, Marcel saw the distinguished connoisseur and man of parts. Ephrussi was editor of the *Gazette des Beaux-Arts* and one of its major contributors, as well as the author of a book-length study of Albrecht Dürer. He was the obverse of Charles Swann in the *Search*, whose fragment of a monograph on Vermeer—a metaphor for his lack of vocation or purpose—is consigned to a drawer. Invited to call at Ephrussi's magnificent new residence in the avenue d'Iéna, Marcel saw Japanese lacquers and screens and paintings by Moreau, Manet, Monet, Renoir, Morrisot, Degas, Pissarro, Puvis de Chavannnes, Sisley, and Mary Cassatt.

Also in 1892 Marcel conceived another of his make-believe passions, this one for a renowned beauty of the Faubourg,

Comtesse Adhéaume de Chévigné, *née* Laure de Sade, a descendant of the Marquis de Sade and boastful about it. When in the *Search* the young Narrator goes mad for Oriane, Duchesse de Guermantes, from whom a gesture of recognition is what he's suddenly living for, he at least has heterosexuality on his side. Readers will remember the great scene at the Opéra when she deigns to acknowledge him: "The Duchess, goddess turned woman, and appearing in that moment a thousand times more lovely, raised towards me the white-gloved hand which had been resting on the balustrade of the box and waved it in token of friendship."[11]

But Marcel never in his life wanted women. He only wanted to want them. The genuine passion of 1892, the year of his majority, was for Edgar Aubert, a brilliant, dashing, athletic, polyglot Genevan newly attached to the Swiss embassy in Paris, whom Marcel met through Billy and who accompanied them to the various *salons* and on walks in the Tuileries. When Marcel asked for a keepsake photo, Edgar readily supplied it with a learned English inscription. Fond of Marcel, he may or may not have understood the extent to which he'd mesmerized someone longing for a deeper response. But back in Switzerland Aubert died suddenly—of appendicitis, as Marcel would later learn while on holiday at Les Frémonts with the Finalys. "He was so sure of returning," Marcel wrote to Billy, "always saying '*In any case* I shall be back next year.' Now those words break my heart. . . . I beg you to write and tell me what his illness was, whether he knew how serious it was, what relations he has left behind, whether they resemble him, a thousand things that would not have interested me before, but are so precious now because they are the last things I shall know of him."[12]

Not quite the last. Several months later, as the season turned, there arrived at boulevard Malesherbes a package containing some sort of memento or souvenir or gift—unspecified in the letter to Billy and now unknowable—from the dead young man. Sent on by his family? Detained in the mails? Unclear. Marcel confided to Billy that the return of spring made him think all the more of Edgar.

* * *

In 1893 he became a fixture at yet another *salon*, that of Madeleine Lemaire at her townhouse at 31, rue Monceau, where the faithful included Loti, France, Lemaître, Bernhardt, Réjane, Mont-Sully, Coquelin, Bartet, and Puvis de Chavannes, in addition to representatives from the old aristocracy and even foreign "royalties," as Odette de Crécy would say: the prince of Wales, the empress of Germany, the king of Sweden, and the queen of the Belgians. Plus the inevitable Princesse Mathilde. And by contrast to Mme Arman de Calillevet's gatherings, at Mme Lemaire's the top drawer of French composers—Saint-Saëns, Massenet, Fauré—were in attendance. Hers was quickly the most talked-about and aspired-to *salon* in all of Europe. Like Mme Verdurin in the *Search*, she subscribed to the religion of modern music and was famous, again like Mme Verdurin, for dismissing without pity from her nucleus those judged dull. Her opinions were arbitrary and could wound; when Marcel had the temerity to praise Gustave Moreau in her presence as an artist of profundity and intellect, she snapped back, "Indeed not! He's a dullard (*un raseur*)!"[13] Mme Lemaire's "raseurs" were the clear source for Mme Verdurin's "ennuyeux," her bores. She liked to paint and draw in the presence of guests—especially roses. Dumas *fils* said that only God had created more roses than Madeleine Lemaire.

In spring Marcel formed a gratifying new friendship with Robert de Flers—a third Robert, whom he now counted, after Robert Dreyfus and Robert de Billy, as indispensable. (Robert de Flers was to know great success in the theater as Gaston Arman de Caillevet's collaborator and to marry the daughter of Victorien Sardou.) Then, on April 13, 1894, at Mme Lemaire's, he met a fourth Robert—this one momentous for Marcel's life and for *In Search of Lost Time:* Count Robert de Montesquiou-Fezensac. Widely seen as the model for Joris-Karl Huysmans's Des Esseintes in *À Rebours*, this outlandish man, thirty-seven when he and Marcel met, sprang from a thousand-year-old Gascony family. A poet of vast self-importance, minor talent, and deep learning, he had a far greater gift for tutelage than for writing. "Like Socrates," says Tadié, "he loved leading epheboi to the Beau Idéal. . . . During this sort of platonic honeymoon, the older man hoped to have found the fervent Roman acolyte that he longed for; [Marcel] was seeking a master, a counsellor, a model for him to imitate and portray, but also someone who could introduce him into aristocratic circles."[14] Marcel and the count were made for each other; but Montesquiou was also renowned, as such mentors are, for feeling sooner or later betrayed, and loved staging operatic breakups; this touchiest of grudge-bearers was admired and feared in equal parts.

His Argentinian secretary, companion, and perhaps lover, Gabriel d'Yturri, saw in him "the whole historic past of France, all the painters, all the books, all the charms."[15] Whistler's portrait of the count in New York's Frick Collection emphasizes a physically imposing presence and, with its what-fools-these-mortals-be glare, captures the count's immense condescension. He had a way of speaking that harked back to the seventeenth century and a knowledge of the history of Europe's aristocracies that was encyclopedic. In these and other respects he may be said to resemble Baron de Charlus in the *Search*. But Montesquiou is a curiosity of passing interest. Proust's imagination transmutes him into a figure on the scale of Don Quixote or Falstaff, a comic giant hedged about with sublime pathos. Here is a sampling of Charlus from early in his and the Narrator's acquaintance: "The circumspect and unceasingly restless expression of those eyes, with all the signs of exhaustion which the heavy pouches beneath them stamped upon his face, however carefully he might compose and regulate it, made one think of some incognito, some disguise assumed by a powerful man in danger, or merely by a dangerous—but tragic—individual. . . . He displayed towards men, and especially young men, a hatred so violent as to suggest that of certain misogynists for women. . . . 'Young scum!' I gathered that the peculiar fault which he found in the young men of the day was their effeminacy. 'They're nothing but women,' he said with scorn."[16] What we learn in the course of the novel is that this hater of young men has been to bed with hundreds of them. When we see him last in *Time Regained*, decrepit and senile, he is in hot pursuit of a gardener. Boundless in vitality, this greatest homosexual in all of literature makes a stark contrast to his supposed model, the all-but-virginal Robert de Montesquiou.

Marcel proceeded to court the count, raving sycophantically in letter after letter. These make unpleasant reading; Charlus's characterization of the young Narrator as "an hysterical little flatterer" comes to mind as an apt description of Marcel himself in this season. By June his social climbing had entered a new phase. At boulevard Malesherbes he hosted an ambitious dinner party of his own, exclusively male, and most all of the guests had the aristocratic "de" in their names. Marcel now felt free to ask the count for an introduction to his cousin the Comtesse Greffulhe, every snob's highest goal. Beyond Élisabeth Greffulhe there was simply nowhere to climb. (Her brutal husband, clearly a key to Basin de Guermantes in the *Search*, is sharply recalled by Cocteau in *Le Passé défini* as a lifelong philanderer betrayed by his last mistress, Mme de La Béraudière, exactly as Basin will be betrayed by Odette in *Time Regained.*)[17] On July 1, at the residence of the Princesse de Wagram, Marcel at last found himself in the presence of his longed-for countesse. "I have never met such a beautiful woman," he afterward enthused to Montesquiou, laying it on thick.[18]

All of this light-minded flitting around would turn out to be essential preparation. Proust was planting in memory the thousands of impressions he would transfigure and make everlasting in the *Search*. One instance: In the drawing room of the Comtesse de Sassine, he encountered the much-lauded young pianist Léon Delafosse, a protégé of Montesquiou. Initially captivated by the young man's beauty, Marcel was then alarmed. He wrote a poem about him called "Falsehoods": "Your hazy eyes, your eager eyes / Your profound eyes alas! are empty." Here is the germ of the virtuoso violinist Charles Morel in the *Search*, a Balzacian amoralist capable of whatever brutality serves his ambitions. Can Delafosse be thus characterized? He seems much less a monster than Charlie. We are told that in certain provincial towns people are afraid to utter the name Morel. Such heightening from life is the true Proustian grotesque; here only Dickens and Dostoyevsky are his equals.

Delafosse's break with Montesquiou, who'd promoted him aggressively in the *beau monde*, was predictably violent when it came—though certainly not life-threatening, as Charlus's rupture with Morel is. In *Les Pas effacés*, his vindictive, posthumously published memoirs, Montesquiou boasts of having dismissed his protégé thus: "Try to ensure that my love for your art is greater than my loathing for yourself."[19] Montesquiou gleefully reports that Delafosse's next patron was an elderly Swiss woman with enormous feet who permitted the young man to play only for duchesses and queens at Monte Carlo. Poor Léon Delafosse, three years Marcel's junior, lived on and on with nothing more to boast of than that Marcel Proust had decanted the lowest villain of the *Search* from him. He died a pauper in 1951 but survives grotesquely, giantly, as Charlie Morel.

* * *

Each Saturday in spring and into summer, Marcel had been taking himself to Auteuil to sit for Jacques-Émile Blanche's portrait of him, nowadays prominently on view at Musée d'Orsay in Paris. "The pure oval visage of an Assyrian," Blanche would afterward say of his handiwork.[20] André Maurois accurately summed up the canvas as "a mixture of the dandified and limp which reminded one, for a brief moment, of Oscar Wilde."[21] But it is Tadié whose reading of the portrait strikes deepest: "In its virginal purity, far removed from his illnesses and all his anxieties, even if they were in the mind, and from all his misdemeanors, is the portrait of Dorian Gray. Time may go by, unhappiness may come, he may be ravaged by asthma, the opportunities to dress in tails with an orchid in his buttonhole become rarer, and the parents who criticized him for going out may die, but one look at Blanche's work and Proust could recapture his youth."[22]

In June Marcel had passed his history and political science examinations without distinction. But in August, to the consternation of Adrien and Jeanne, he flunked the second half of the law test. A drillmaster named Monnot was summoned to tutor the unzealous student. Jeanne and Adrien saw young men all around their son making careers. Billy for instance had been seconded to the French embassy in Berlin. That their Marcel was unlikely to do anything of the kind was probably clear to them. His refrain for some time had been that literature was all he cared about and all he was good for. He had written fifteen pieces for *Le Banquet* and was beginning to fancy them between covers. In July and August he contributed nine sketches to *La Revue Blanche*, a distinguished journal for which Debussy wrote the music column. "I still believe that anything I do outside of literature and philosophy will be just so much *temps perdu*,"[23] he wrote to his father, weirdly presaging the noun-and-adjective combination—*temps perdu*, meaning both time lost and time wasted—that was to organize his mature thinking and give his masterpiece its title.

The highlight of summer 1893 must have been his stay with

Adrien and Robert at 9, Boulevard Malesherbes.
Bibliothèque Nationale de France

Louis de La Salle, a friend from childhood, at Pension Vernguth, Saint-Moritz, at this time Europe's most fashionable resort, where the two fished for trout and went hiking. From the summit of Alp Grüm Marcel saw clear to Italy, his heart's desire from childhood, though this was the nearest he would get for another seven years. From Saint-Moritz, he proceeded by himself to Évian-les-Bains and from Évian to Trouville, where his mother—overwrought with anxiety, as always—awaited him. Throughout that summer Marcel worked on his largest composition to date, a novella called "The Indifferent One," about a man who can find satisfaction only with prostitutes. In September he published "Melancholy Journey of Mme Breyves" in the *Revue Blanche*, where in December "Before Night," an explicitly homosexual story, had appeared, to no great effect. "Melancholy Journey" would be excluded from *Pleasures and Days*, a debut three years off, but already Marcel was confiding to friends his wish to publish such a collection.

"In spite of the obvious—perhaps too obvious—flirtations with attractive young women like Jeanne Pouquet," writes Carter, "and occasional rumors about girlfriends or cousins he might marry, nothing indicates that Marcel or his parents ever considered marriage a serious prospect."[24] The new object of Marcel's deeper feelings was Willie Heath, a dashing English cousin of Edgar Aubert's, though Willie would die as suddenly as his cousin, strange to say, and within a matter of months of meeting Marcel. The date of death, October 3, 1893, and cause, dysentery, are all we know of him apart from a sketch Proust would offer in the dedicatory epistle of *Pleasures and Days*, published only in 1895: "Mornings in the Bois I often found you, standing but in repose, awaiting me under the trees with the pensive elegance of one of Van Dyck's noblemen. . . . Those were the days when we formed our dream, very nearly our project, of living more and more for each other, surrounded by a circle of magnanimous men and women, far from folly, vice, and wickedness, and safe from the slings and arrows of the vulgar." His original intent had been to dedicate *Pleasures and Days* to the memory of Aubert too, but the young man's parents indignantly refused, perhaps having read Marcel's letters to their son. These have never come to light and it is likely that the Auberts destroyed them.

One week after Willie's death Marcel received his law degree and commenced a fortnight's internship with attorney Gustave Brunet. It was to be the whole of his law career. By December a new vocation had budded. Modeling himself on

Saint-Beuve, Leconte de Lisle, and Anatole France—all librarians in their time—Marcel took a position as "unremunerated assistant" at the Bibliothèque Mazarine: a sop to the parents, and there is scant record of his turning up for work. For what he was bent on was what Tadié calls the "career one cannot be sacked from, literature." It was in this period that he produced his best work to date, "Ambitions and Tastes of Bouvard and Pécuchet," destined for *Pleasures and Days.* In this essay many received ideas are mocked, particularly those pertaining to Jews: "They all have hooked noses, exceptional intelligence, a heart that is base and only concerned with interest rates. . . . What is more, they form a sort of vast secret society, like the Jesuits and Freemasons. Against alleged enemies they have laid up an inexhaustible treasure, one knows not where."[25]

* * *

On May 22, 1894, at Mme Lemaire's, Marcel met the vibrant young composer Reynaldo Hahn, who'd been invited to perform his settings of Verlaine's *Gray Songs.* Three years Marcel's junior, born in Caracas to a Venezuelan Catholic mother and German Jewish father and brought up in Paris, he would be a great passion of Marcel's and, after that, his most lasting intimate—the only friend allowed, in later years, to drop by unannounced. Having entered the Conservatoire at eleven to study composition with Jules Massenet and others, at thirteen Reynaldo had set Victor Hugo's "If my verses had wings," an air still heard today. He promptly introduced Marcel to the star-studded *salon* of Trieste-born Ernesta de Herschel Stern, wife of Louis Stern, a leading Jewish banker. Their sumptuous hospitality at 68, rue du Faubourg Saint-Honoré would be yet another source for the Verdurin milieu in *In Search of Lost Time*—with, as usual, contrasts as salient as similarities: Mme Verdurin's faithful are relative nobodies; Mme Stern counted heads of state and leading artists among her clan. Gustave Verdurin is an idle, henpecked fool; Louis Stern had organized payment of the indemnity owed to Germany following the Franco-Prussian War and afterward helped to capitalize France's development of Tunisia.

In August the two young men grew closer at Château de Réveillon, Mme Lemaire's country retreat in the Marne. It seems certain that they first made love under her roof. From the start, these two made a poignant couple: At twenty Hahn was preparing commissions for the Opéra Comique. At twenty-three Marcel had yet to seek a publisher for his miscellany of magazine pieces that, in homage to their hostess that summer, and in homage to the love consummated at her house, he'd decided to call *Le Château de Réveillon*.

Fashionable society had been available to Reynaldo from early youth. Where Marcel was wide-eyed, Reynaldo was smoothly in his element, untroubled by the self-consciousness that dogged his lover. Marcel was doubtless a brilliant talker—as amateurish or stalled artists sometimes are, squandering what ought to be held in reserve—but no one considered him a rising star. Tadié has seen an unpublished letter from Reynaldo to Suzette—Mme Lemaire's daughter, who had innocently fallen for Marcel, and to whom Marcel had not so innocently responded as a cover for his involvement with Reynaldo—in which the composer writes: "His expansive nature leads him to be open-hearted and he then has to become more introverted so as to avoid the little things his delicate heart must dread."[26] Years later Reynaldo said that no one then detected the least glimmer of genius in him, only a stymied intelligence.

Much of Hahn's diary—the holy grail of Proust biographers—remains sealed until 2036, so one must speculate. But it does seem clear that Reynaldo was Marcel's first episode of reciprocated love—after years of wondering what such an experience would be. The musical prodigy addressed alternately as "dear child" and "my master" was who he'd longed for, body and soul, someone younger than himself but fully formed, manly and complete. The mature Hahn recollected by Cocteau in his *Portraits-souvenirs* is the same as the twenty-year-old at Réveillon in that summer of 1894: "Whether at Madeleine Lemaire's or in his room at the mysterious Hôtel des Réservoirs at Versailles, Reynaldo would sing, cigarette locked into one side of his mouth, exquisite voice purling from the other, eyes tilted heavenward."[27] In another unpublished letter to their hostess Reynaldo wrote: "How indulgent you are toward us, we who are such lunatics and so badly brought up. . . . What other woman or great artist would put up, as you do, with the quirks and the company of two old-fashioned young men."[28] "Old-fashioned" here means a good deal and it is certain that Mme Lemaire was aware of the nature of the attachment.

* * *

That summer a debt-ridden major in the French army, Ferdinand Walsin-Esterhazy, had presented himself to General Maximilian von Schwartzkoppen, military attaché at the German embassy in Paris, and offered to sell classified French secrets pertaining to current arms developments and planned deployment of forces. But unknown to Schwartzkoppen, the French military's Statistics Section (an anodyne name for their intelligence and counterintelligence division) had a spy within the German embassy, a cleaning woman named Marie Bastian who regularly collected information from the wastepaper baskets. One such document would change French history—a handwritten, torn-up, unsigned piece of onionskin paper that, when pieced back together, enumerated the items Esterhazy had offered for sale. This *bordereau*, as it came to be called, delivered by Mme Bastian to the men of the Statistics Section on September 25, was immediately recognized as proof of a highly placed traitor in their midst. Twenty days later Captain Alfred Dreyfus, sole Jewish officer trainee on the General Staff, was asked by Lieutenant-Colonel Armand Mercier du Paty de Clam to take down a dictation that was, in fact, the words of the *bordereau*. This handwriting sample was compared to that of the treasonous document. They were declared identical; Dreyfus was arrested on the spot and taken to the Cherche-midi prison. On October 31 *Le Soir* identified him by name as the officer charged with treason, unleashing a virulent campaign in the major antisemitic papers: *La Libre Parole*, *L'Éclair*, *Le Petit Journal*, *L'Intransigeant*, and others. A journalism of explicitly political loathing—the argument that "real" Frenchmen were threatened by the presence in their midst of Jews, whose loyalty was to one another and who were therefore likely to betray France—had developed in high-, middle-, and lowbrow versions. As its greatest contemporary student, Bernard Lazare, would write in his book *Antisemitism: Its History and Causes:* "The hostility against the Jews, which was formerly rooted in sentiment, now became philosophical. . . . The new anti-Jews wanted to be able to explain their hatred—i. e. to adorn it. Anti-Judaism had become anti-Semitism."[29]

The antisemitic press was clearly being fed inflammatory information by sources within the Statistics Section. On December 19 the court-martial of Alfred Dreyfus began behind covered windows. On December 22 the so-called *dossier secret*, containing manufactured documents incriminating to Dreyfus, and a memorandum explaining their supposed pertinence to the case, was delivered to the judges by Paty de Clam, who had concocted the memorandum on orders of General Auguste Mercier, minister of war. Dreyfus's lawyer was not informed of this new "evidence," a criminal violation of the defendant's rights. On the basis of weak arguments for the similarity of his handwriting to that of the *bordereau*, buttressed by the *dossier secret*, all three judges found Dreyfus guilty. He was sentenced to degradation, deportation and imprisonment for life at Devil's Island off the coast of French Guyana. On January 5, in the courtyard of the École militaire, Dreyfus had the braid torn from his epaulettes and cap and the buttons cut from his uniform; his sword was taken from him and broken. A jeering crowd shouted "Death to the Jew!" and "Judas!" and "Traitor!" Harder to hear was the voice of the humiliated captain crying out: "Soldiers, an innocent man is being degraded. Soldiers, an innocent man is being dishonored. *Vive la France! Vive l'Armée!*" Leading anti-semites who witnessed the ceremony that day would wax eloquent about it. Here is Léon Daudet, soon to be a great friend of Marcel's, reporting in *Le Figaro:* "His was the color of treason. His face was ashen, without relief, base, without appearance of remorse, foreign, to be sure, debris of the ghetto. . . . This wretch is not French. . . . He plotted our disaster, but his crime has exalted us."[30]

Chapter Three

On a mild evening in April 1895 an episode occurred that took root in Marcel's imagination. Owing to Mme Lemaire's insistence that he accompany her to something called the "pink cotillion," Marcel arrived late for his usual rendezvous with Reynaldo and did not find him at the appointed place. In a fever, he rushed from café to restaurant to bar in search of his beloved. "Wait for my boy, lose him, find him, lose him twice as much on hearing that he had come back to get me . . ." he writes the next day to Reynaldo, "wait two minutes for him or make him wait for five, that for me is the true, throbbing, profound tragedy, which I shall perhaps write some day and which in the meantime I am living."[1] He would indeed write this comi-tragedy. Its title would be "Swann in Love," the second part of *Swann's Way*, in which a desperate Charles Swann, finding Odette de Crécy neither at the Verdurins' nor at Prévost's, their usual spot, searches frantically for her in every other restaurant along the boulevards. Who is the beloved with, if not with him? Every guess is unbearable. It is then that he knows love has mastered him, love's proof being the jealousy it engenders.

In *The Captive*, volume five of the *Search*, the Narrator will say of lovers: "Even when you hold them in your hands, such persons are fugitives. To understand the emotions which they arouse, and which others even better looking do not, we must recognize that they are not immobile but in motion, and add to their person a sign corresponding to that which in physics denotes speed."[2] This sublime pair of sentences, with their compressed wisdom and revelatory metaphor, are a good way down the Proustian path. The bright young man will need to become a genius before such glories can be written. But in the first blush of love for Reynaldo, Marcel did manage a premonitory truthfulness in which his mature understanding, if not the mature force of his style, may be glimpsed. In "A Critique of Hope in the Light of Love" he captures the instability of all things, love especially: "No sooner has a future moment become the present than it is stripped of its charms, to be found again, it is true. . . on the paths of memory."[3]

In early September, following a stay with Mme Lemaire at her Normandy residence in Dieppe, the young men journeyed to Belle-Isle-en-Mer, off the Brittany coast, to visit Sarah Bernhardt at her newly purchased fortress. After meeting the great actress briefly, Marcel fell ill of an intestinal virus, and he and Reynaldo retreated to Beg-Meil on the mainland, registering at Hôtel Fermont, a converted farmhouse where their flyblown room (even the hotel stationary was flyblown) cost two francs a night and the amenities did not include basic plumbing. Reynaldo signed the register as "musicien," no more than the fact; Marcel announced himself, aspiration darting ahead of achievement, as "homme de lettres." "The apple trees come down to the sea," he wrote to Montesquiou from Beg-Meil, "and the smell of cider mingles with that of seaweed. The mixture of poetry and sensuality is just about right for me."[4] When he was strong enough, and with the touristic zeal of the young, Marcel and Reynaldo explored the ancient Breton towns and harshly beautiful landscapes: Quimper, Concarneau, Pointe du Raz, Pointe de Penmarch. Brittany seemed to have a catalytic effect on him, and it was at this moment that he wrote the earliest sketches for *Jean Santeuil*, that failure paving the way for *In Search of Lost Time*.

Marcel would never revisit Brittany, nor would he know again the romantic bliss of the enchanted days spent there. Here is Jean Santeuil bedding down in a passage that almost certainly registers the experience of physical love with Reynaldo at Hôtel Fermont: "Then it would be time to go to sleep in the box beds, the dark night filled with strange dreams that are interrupted when the noise of the storms rattles the windowpanes and awakens the sleepers, with their soft, drowsy kisses, arms wrapped around each other's neck and legs entwined, their kisses that deepen the silence, as the wind hurls itself against the casements, seizes the roof and sets the chimney damper sighing, when a head raises itself from the pillow, without disturbing the encircling arms to listen to the noise . . . then plunges down again and shelters beneath sheets for warmth and affection within, while outside all is cold and hostile."[5] This has the authority of bliss remembered. There is no trace of any such eroticism in the *Search*.

By mid-September he had gone on to Trouville and Maman. Mme Straus and retinue were nearby at Le Clos des Mûriers, her country estate. Under the spell of Reynaldo, Marcel wrote three stories: "The Death of Baldassare Silvande, Viscount of Sylvania," "The End of Jealousy," and, most significant, "The Confession of a Young Girl," in which there is a first iteration of two linked themes, small-scale here but destined to grow to epic size—the mother's goodnight kiss and the child's decline of will: "She would come and bid me goodnight when I was in bed," says the girl who narrates, "an old custom which she had stopped, because it afforded me so much pleasure and so much sorrow: I was unable to go to sleep because I kept calling her back to say goodnight to me again, and eventually not daring to do so, which only made me feel that desperate need all the more—I would constantly be inventing new pretexts: my burning hot pillow which needed to be turned over, my frozen feet which only she could warm in her hands."[6] In the *Search* the Narrator will similarly date the inexorable (as he believes) decline of his will to the trauma of the longed-for maternal kiss.

Marcel could blunder, in society as in love, by trying too hard. One particular lapse led him, in a gauche try at impressing Montesquiou's cousin Mme de Brantes, to write to her on violet paper with gold ink, the gesture of a fop. Well, wasn't he? Despite flashes of brilliance in his published work to date, Marcel seemed to be confirming Gide's original judgment of him. The necessary detour through high society would continue for many more years, though sometimes rewardingly. It was on December 18, one day before the closed court-martial of Dreyfus began, that Reynaldo had taken Marcel to the residence of Mme Arthur Baignères and introduced him to M. and Mme Alphonse Daudet. The near-mythic author of *Letters from My Windmill* and *Tartarin of Tarrascon* (a favorite of Marcel's youth) was doubtless the most self-made of contemporary authors; an impoverished youth from Nîmes, whose father had gone bankrupt selling silks, he'd come to Paris in the 1850s and made the hard climb to preeminence. The Daudets and their children would become a second family to Proust. Finding in them, as in the Finalys, more suitable consanguinity than his own kin could provide—the usual callow story, youth being the season for such emotions—he fell for the Daudets much as the protagonists of *The Gar-*

den of the Finzi-Continis and *Brideshead Revisited* fall. A clearer case of what Freud named "family romance" would be hard to find.

Daudet had only three years to live when Marcel met him. Tabes dorsalis, a consequence of tertiary syphilis, would carry the great writer off at fifty-eight. His late masterpiece, *La Doulou*, is among the most searching accounts of illness ever written. But it was Daudet's valor that seems to have impressed Marcel more than his work: "He had no sooner taken to his bed than his pains became unbearable and, every evening, he swallowed a bottle of chloral in order to get to sleep. I could not understand, however, how he managed to continue to write. I particularly remembered how the pains I suffered, so slight by comparison to his that he would probably have looked upon them as a respite, had made me indifferent to other people, to life, to everything outside my own wretched body, upon which my mind remained obstinately fixed, just as a sick person in bed keeps his face turned to the wall."[7] Youth notwithstanding, Marcel's recurrent asthma attacks and bronchitis raised the specter of invalidism, and in Daudet's decline he feared to have glimpsed his own future.

* * *

Marcel's appetite for music grew by what it fed on. Transported the previous year at the Paris premiere of Verdi's *Otello*, Marcel now attended the Opéra's hugely successful new production of *Tannhaüser*. (An interesting sidelight on the history of taste: Thirty years earlier it had been booed there.) At Mme Stern's he came to know Gabriel Fauré and César Franck, among living composers his two favorites. Fauré's *Ballade* would be a model for the slow movement of Vinteuil's sonata in "Swann in Love"—the "national anthem" of Swann's love for Odette—and Fauré would be one of those elder eminences, like Anatole France, Daudet, and others, whom Marcel seemed to collect. "Then," writes Tadié, "once Vinteuil had been created, [Fauré] disappeared from the life and correspondence of the person who had taken from him all that he needed for his work. This journey from youth . . . to maturity is one of prescience to realization. In this, as in everything, when Proust felt passionate about somebody else's creation, it was a sign that he was foreseeing his own work."[8]

At Dieppe that summer he met Saint-Saëns and would publish an article on him for *Le Gaulois*. Entranced by his opus 75, the first Sonata for Piano and Violin, he would ask Reynaldo frequently to play "la petite phrase," as the two of them called it, from the first movement. In *Jean Santeuil* the little phrase will be explicitly attributed: "He had recognized that little phrase in Saint-Saëns' sonata which he used to ask [his lover Françoise] to play almost every evening in the heyday of their love and which she used to play endlessly, ten or twenty times over."[9]

He wrote to Suzette Lemaire in May of 1895: "The essential purpose of music is to awaken in us the mysterious depths of our soul (which literature, painting and sculpture cannot express)—depths that begin at the point where all the arts aimed at the finite stop and at which science stops too, and which may thus be described as religious."[10] Painting, also, was much on his mind. Essays on Rembrandt and Chardin, written at this time but only posthumously published, are the source for ideas that will reach their final form in the *Search*. The essay on Chardin in particular is a sketch of what will be the aesthetic of Elstir, Proust's consummate painter: "The pleasure you get from his painting of a room where a woman sits sewing, a pantry, a kitchen, a sideboard, is the pleasure—seized on the wing, redeemed from the transient, ascertained, pondered, perpetuated—that he got from the sight of a sideboard, a kitchen, a room where a woman sat sewing."[11]

On October 29 "The Death of Baldassare Silvande," Proust's strongest story to date, appeared in *La Revue hebdoma-*

daire, dedicated "to Reynaldo Hahn, poet, singer, and musician." He was paid 150 francs, evidently the first money he'd earned from writing. So it was perhaps with the feeling of being a man of letters at last that he took himself on November 14 to a dinner party at the Daudets', where all hope of literary conversation perished when the talk turned rabidly antisemitic. Among those present were François Coppée, Edmond de Goncourt, Maurice Barrès, and Charles-Louis Phillippe. Goncourt recorded the evening in his diary, where the drift of the talk went unmentioned; there would have been nothing for him to take exception to, as rabid antisemitism was Goncourt's distinct predisposition. There is no evidence that, listening to these views, Marcel did anything but hold his tongue. It is a familiar trial of youth to know oneself better than one's elders but be fearful of standing up to them. Did he wonder why these exquisitely refined people failed to remember that his mother was Jewish? Next day in a remarkable letter to Reynaldo—a half-Jew like himself—Marcel pilloried the evening: "They account for character and genius by physical habits or race. . . . Even more astounding in Daudet, a pure and brilliant intellect shining through the mists and storms of his nerves, a small star on the sea."[12] Marcel had fallen in, not for the last time, with some of the most distinguished Jew-haters in all of Europe.

Six months later when Montesquiou gave similar offense, instead of reporting it to Reynaldo Marcel responded to the malefactor himself, and splendidly: "Dear Sir, Yesterday I did not answer the question that you put to me about the Jews. For this very simple reason: though I am a Catholic, like my father and brother, my mother is Jewish. I am sure you understand that this is reason enough for me to refrain from such discussions." He added, in a telling phrase that perhaps summed up his feelings about the maternal heritage, that he was "not free to have the ideas I might otherwise have on the subject."[13] This choice of words, so tense with ambivalence, is Marcel's deepest avowal about the Jews: He was not at liberty to dislike them.

In any case, relations with Montesquiou were by this time starting their long decline. It had come to the count's attention that Marcel, a gifted mimic, was entertaining gatherings with impersonations of him. Marcel defended himself by claiming —dubiously—that the mimicry was in homage, a plea Montesquiou was not inclined to accept.

On Christmas Eve, 1896, the young author's most distinguished supporter, Anatole France, was elected to the Académie Française; but from the day of his induction, he refused to set foot in the Institut de France, rightly regarding it as a hotbed of anti-Dreyfusardism. Little read today, France was a major figure in his time and certainly a key to Bergotte, the great novelist of the *Search*. Kindly by all accounts, he had proved instrumental in getting Proust's first book published in the summer of 1896 and contributed a laudatory preface that appeared beforehand on the front page of *Le Gaulois*. Having replaced the working title of *Chateau de Réveillon* with *Pleasures and Days*, a variation on Hesiod's *Works and Days*, Marcel launched his little collection of *nouvelles*, poems, *poèmes en prose*, portraits, and sketches. It entered the Parisian shops quietly, very quietly, on June 12. Lavishly produced by Calmann-Lévy and with illustrations by Mme Lemaire (whose dilatoriness had postponed publication), it cost thirteen francs, fifty centimes—which was too much. Sales were virtually nonexistent. In the *Revue Encyclopédique* Charles Maurras declared that "the new generation will have to get used to relying on this young writer." And in *La Revue Blanche* Léon Blum's praise was generous and prescient. (He either ignored or was unaware of Proust's negative review of him several years earlier in *Le Banquet*.) On the other hand, a scurrilous litterateur named Jean Lorrain used the book's appearance to launch an attack in *Le Journal* on Marcel and his association with Montesquiou, whose place in society and letters Lorrain greatly envied. As well, clever disparagement of *Pleasures and Days* and its author was circulating among Marcel's friends, one of whom offered up a mock advertisement: "Proust—A foreword by M. France, four francs . . . Paintings by Mme Lemaire, four francs . . . Music by Reynaldo Hahn, four francs . . . Prose by myself, one franc . . . A few of my poems, fifty centimes . . ."[14] Most grievous of all was Jacques Bizet and others staging a three-night run, in Jacques's apartment, of *La Vie parisienne*, their send-up of the book.

Proust wouldn't even have the distinction of being a forgotten writer if he'd stopped after this first offering; outside of certain drawing rooms, he'd never have been known at all. A fin-de-siècle product if ever there was one—languid, epicene, naughty—*Pleasures and Days* featured twilit landscapes, tormented lesbians, jealousies only death can cure. One of Proust's best critics, André Maurois, would accurately characterize it as "perfunctory, over-ornamented, inexpert, and charming."[15] Certainly a talent for fraught atmospheres and dark insinuations is present; but there is little in this debut of what we think of as Proustian. (Nor in "The Indifferent One," the workmanlike but rather lifeless story excluded from the collection.) In 1922, shortly after Proust's death, Gide would write, knowing of the wonders to come: "When I now reread *Pleasures and Days,* the qualities of this gentle book, published in 1896, seem to me so startling that I am astonished that we were not dazzled in the first place. But today our eye has been alerted and everything which, subsequently, we may have been able to admire in Marcel Proust's recent books we can now recognize here in a place where at first we had not known to look."[16] In homage to Proust, so recently dead, Gide overestimates the promise *Pleasures and Days* held. Alongside the startling *Notebooks of*

André Walter, his own debut at age twenty-one, Proust's at twenty-six seems an amateurish production.

* * *

On June 20, 1896, at Marcel's insistence, he and Reynaldo ("you whom along with Maman I love best in all the world") sealed a solemn covenant to tell each other about everything in their lives, including (or especially) their sexual desires. Such pacts are predictably the prelude to estrangement. The beginning of wisdom is to understand that your lover's inner life is not yours to know. Bargains in which each pledges to tell the other everything are the sure path to mutual recrimination. Marcel's jealous drive to possess inwardly whomever he loved was to be repeated again and again, and hurried each attachment to its end. Predictably, he and Reynaldo quarreled and decided not to spend their August holiday together. Instead Marcel traveled with his mother to Mont-Dore, a spa for asthmatics in the Auvergne, where he got no better relief than from the Espic medicated cigarettes or Legras and Escouflaire powders he inhaled at home.

It was at Mont-Dore that he settled down in earnest to *Jean Santeuil*, reporting "110 grandes pages" to his mother by the second week of September, though also confessing an inability "to conceive it as a whole." All the same, he was by now in possession of an artistic credo, formulated that summer in an impressive essay, "Against Obscurity," and published in *La Revue Blanche*. He had allied himself with the classicism of Anatole France's *La Vie littéraire* and against Mallarmé and his circle (Valéry, Régnier). Mallarmé's riposte, "Mystery in literature," appeared six weeks later in the same publication. It was a signal moment. Proust was shaking off the mystique of Symbolism and turning to the realist art that was his calling.

A final love letter to Reynaldo reveals the dawning sense that jealous desire forged into unjealous friendship is the best to be hoped for: "My dearest little one, you would be very wrong to think that my silence is the sort that is preparing for oblivion. It is of the kind that is like a loyal cinder that keeps tenderness intact and burning. My affection for you remains the same and I can more easily see that it is a fixed star when I see it in the same position after so many fires have taken place."[17]

The truth was that he was in love anew, this time with eighteen-year-old Lucien Daudet, whom he'd first observed two years earlier as a beautiful silent youth at the Daudets' dinner table. By the autumn of 1896 they were sharing secrets, laughing hysterically and being as great a trial as young people in love usually are. Montesquiou in particular was irked, suspecting correctly that the *fou rire* was sometimes at his expense. As a New Year's gift Marcel presented his new beloved with an expensive eighteenth-century carved ivory box. Cost would never be an impediment, and at about this time there occurred in boulevard Malesherbes a family scene about Marcel's spending habits. He got into a rage and smashed one of his mother's cherished vases, and also perhaps the glass in a door he slammed behind him. From his room that evening he dispatched a note of apology to both parents. Jeanne's tender response included this: "From now on let the broken glass be what it is in the synagogue—a symbol of indissoluble union."[18] Shortly thereafter, Proust would narrate a slightly transformed version of this episode in *Jean Santeuil.* And many years later he would tell it very differently to Céleste Albaret, claiming that the cause was Jeanne's having purchased gray gloves for him instead of the cream-colored pair with which he wanted to impress a lady he was ostentatiously courting.[19]

Gloves were not the issue. What had upset Jeanne was a studio photograph of a very effeminate Lucien gazing amorously at her son. (Robert de Flers is also pictured.) There exist, in a private collection, fifty letters from Marcel to Lucien; these remain, like the Hahn diaries, unavailable to scholars. But the testimony of someone who did see one of them makes clear that Lucien and Marcel "were not bored"—that is, not unaroused—"when they met."[20] The young men had become lovers and Jeanne, in the way of mothers, knew perfectly well what her son was up to.

On February 3, 1897, Jean Lorrain launched a second missile in *Le Journal*, charging Marcel with "delicacy" and other deficits in manliness. Lorrain, an outlandish queen himself, had a history of impugning the virility of men he envied. His insinuating final sentence—"Rest assured that for his next book M. Marcel Proust will obtain a preface from M. Alphonse Daudet . . . who will not be able to refuse this preface either to Mme Lemaire or to his son Lucien"—required that honor be satisfied. The appointed date was February 6, the place Ermitage de Villebon, Meudon forest. But the duel had to be scheduled for afternoon, Marcel insisted, owing to his habit of rising late. At Meudon shots were duly exchanged. Nobody was hurt. No handshake was offered afterward. The harmless outcome was announced next day in *Le Figaro*, *Le Gaulois*, and *Le Journal*. Proust would count the duel among his fondest memories.[21]

But a willingness to risk life and limb for Lucien's honor was evidently not enough to sustain his passion for the boy. By spring of 1898 relations had cooled. Several years later Marcel would write to Antoine Bibesco that his love sicknesses were of twelve to eighteen months' duration, "a period after which such affections, in medical terms, always recede and die away."[22] This was to prove an accurate understanding of himself, as of the great lovers of the *Search:* Swann, Saint Loup, Charlus, and the Narrator, all of whose savage passions fade as if according to a timetable.

Marcel's next fascination was Grant Duff, also known as Douglas Ainslie, a Scotsman friendly with Pater, Wilde, and Henry James. He left a vivid portrait of Marcel at this stage: "I shall always see Proust, the velvet collar of his overcoat drawn up over his ears, arriving late at the Café Weber. He hastened to say immediately that he intended staying only a moment, but that moment stretched out indefinitely, and he would stay until everyone had left, so that the evening seemed to go on longer and longer. . . . Proust needed to feel that he had an impatient cab driver beside him to give of his best."[23] Marcel would invite Ainslie back to boulevard Malesherbes, just around the corner from Café Weber, to gossip about those they'd been with. Only after three in the morning, says Ainslie, would he reveal the deeper secrets of his heart.

The gossip also included English letters. Ainslie told him something Pater had said: "I don't believe Ruskin can have discovered more things in St. Mark's than I did!"[24] As a Paterian, not a Ruskinian, Ainslie thought this very fine, but it seems to have exasperated Proust, who'd been swayed to Ruskin—without knowing his work; almost nobody in France did at this time—on account of a series of articles by Robert de La Sizeranne (afterward a book, *John Ruskin et la religion de la beauté*) in the *Revue des Deux Mondes*. It launched Marcel in the direction of aesthetics and away from the episodic, themeless accumulation of his novel in progress. This instinct for Ruskin, Marcel's intuitions about what was in those untranslated books he could not read, was of a piece with his other English and American preferences: French translations of Emerson, Dickens, Carlyle, George Eliot, Stevenson, and Hardy had all left their mark on him. Ill at ease, as "Against Obscurity" announced, with the Symbolist revolution, Marcel had hearkened instead to the great moralists of English-speaking lands. He would, as it turned out, consecrate nine vital years to the author of *Modern Painters* and *The Stones of Venice*, abandoning his thousand-page *Santeuil* in order to work for the greater glory of John Ruskin. Capable of reciting, with ghastly pronunciation, long passages by heart in English, he would go on to translate (relying on his mother's excellent command of English) first *The Bible of*

Amiens and then *Sesame and Lilies.* These labors in a poorly known language seem to have been exactly what he required in order to bring to birth a style of his own. "Such voluntary subjugation," he would write, "is the beginning of freedom. There is no better way of becoming aware of what one feels oneself than by trying to recreate in oneself that which a master has experienced. In this profound effort that we make, it is our own way of thinking, together with the master's, that we bring to light."[25]

Chapter Four

Marcel and his friends could not have known what was unfolding at the Statistics Section that spring, summer, and autumn. In March 1896 Mme Bastian—"the normal channel"—had handed on to Lieutenant Colonel Georges Picquart, new chief of the Section, a second remarkable document retrieved from Schwartzkoppen's trash bin, the so-called *petit bleu*, an express letter addressed in his hand to Esterhazy but evidently thrown out instead of being sent.[1] Picquart, who would prove heroic and self-sacrificing in the Affair, inferred from this that the traitor must be Esterhazy, not Dreyfus. As proof he obtained a sample of Esterhazy's handwriting and confirmed that it was identical—not similar but identical—to that of the *bordereau.* Armed with this certainty, Picquart then reviewed the documents of the *dossier secret* and saw that there was nothing in them of probative value. This was the turning point. Owing to Picquart the eventual vindication of Alfred Dreyfus became inevitable, despite dogged rear-guard actions by the army to spare itself a judicial review of the 1894 court-martial.

On May 16 Émile Zola published in *Le Figaro* his fierce and dazzling article "Pour les Juifs," the most powerful account to date of the growing phenomenon of politicized Jew-hatred in France: "People, some of them friends of mine, tell me that they cannot abide Jews; that they shudder with repugnance upon shaking hands with them. . . . Embrace the Jews," he implores France, "in order that we may enrich ourselves with their qualities. They do not lack for them." It is a peril to the nation, he writes, "that such a return of fanaticism, urging even religious war, should have arisen in our time, in our great Paris, among our good people."

One evening in October of 1897 Joseph Reinach, who represented Digne, capital of Alps-de-Haute-Provence, in the Chambre des Députés, had made the case at Mme Straus's *salon* that it was Commandant Esterhazy who'd written the *bordereau.* Among those eminences present, Degas, Gustave Schlumberger, Jules Lemaître, and Jean-Louis Forain denounced Reinach on the spot and forever left 104, rue de Miromesnil. Mme Straus's *salon* would henceforth be a center of Dreyfusard advocacy with Reinach as leader. In November a Parisian securities dealer, J. de Castro, upon seeing the published facsimile of the *bordereau*, recognized the handwriting as that of his client Esterhazy and was able to corroborate Picquart's conclusion of the previous year.

It was at this moment that the military became actively complicit in efforts to hide the identity of the actual traitor; Major Joseph Henry, who had perjured himself at the court-marital of 1894 by giving testimony against Dreyfus, concocted a piece of false evidence later known as the *faux Henry*—a letter purportedly from the Italian military attaché to Schwartzkoppen incriminating Dreyfus definitively—and handed it to General Gonse, deputy chief of staff of the army. A month later he began a series of successful attempts to smear General Picquart—incorruptible throughout, whatever his private distaste for Jews—as the puppet of Dreyfus's brother, Mathieu.

On November 13 a man with an exceptional reputation for statesmanship, Auguste Scheurer-Kestner, vice president of the Senate, published a letter in *Le Figaro* declaring that Dreyfus was innocent and that the true culprit was known to the Statistics Section. It was this letter that finally brought on the national crisis, Zola following up in *Le Figaro* with a defense of Scheurer-Kestner in the last sentence of which he coined the *cri de bataille* of Dreyfusism: "*La verité est en marche, et rien n'arrêtera*"—Truth is on the march, and nothing will stop it. On December 13 his pamphlet "Letter to Youth," a clarion to the Latin Quarter, went on sale.

It was three days later that Alphonse Daudet, no friend to Dreyfusards or Jews—though he'd been warmly hospitable to Marcel from their first meeting—died after his long struggle with syphilis. "Adieux," Proust's eulogy, was published in *La Presse*. One wonders about relations between Dreyfusard Marcel and the antisemitic Daudet household at this point. Like everyone, they would have seen on young Marcel's face the map of Zion, and he spoke readily about his mother's religious background. Yet somehow Léon, virulently bigoted all his life, would be the dedicatée of *The Guermantes Way*. One must conclude that the Daudets' contempt for Jewish blood did not extend to Marcel. By the same token, Proust's loathing for anti-Dreyfusards seems to have exempted the Daudets.

From the day Scheurer-Kestner's letter appeared in *Le Figaro* Marcel campaigned on behalf of Dreyfus. Was this because he felt Jewish? Certainly not. Proust saw himself as what he was: the non-Jewish son of a Jewish mother. The Dreyfus Affair was for him, first and last, a clear-cut miscarriage of justice that demanded reversal. In this he was like most of the Jews, half-Jews, and baptized Jews who rallied to the cause in

1897 and 1898; they did so not because Dreyfus was Jewish but because he was innocent. (However, as Léon Blum pointed out in his *Souvenirs sur l'affaire*, the majority of acculturated Jews did not become Dreyfusard; they tended to remain silent, many of them convinced of the Captain's guilt.)[2]

About Jeanne's response to the Affair we know virtually nothing. But that it roiled her household is not in doubt. On January 13, 1897, Zola's seismic "J'accuse . . . !" appeared in Georges Clemenceau's *L'Aurore*. In a state of exalted indignation France's greatest living novelist argued for the culpability of Esterhazy, notwithstanding his recent "vindication" in a shabby court-martial behind closed doors, and denounced those on the General Staff guilty of shielding the traitor. Zola moreover challenged the army to prosecute him for having named names. One day later Clemenceau ran a "Manifesto of the Intellectuals" in support of Dreyfus and Zola. Among the several hundred signatories were Marcel and Robert Proust. Their enraged father did not speak to either for two weeks. Marcel himself had obtained Anatole France's signature for *L'Aurore* and for this reason called himself—absurdly—"the first Dreyfusard."

Three weeks after the appearance of "J'accuse . . . !" Zola's first trial on charges of defaming the army began. Despite the considerable difficulty of rising at a respectable hour, Marcel managed to get himself to the courtroom gallery. Like Jean Santeuil, he would start "early from home so as to arrive in good time for the Zola trial and the Cour d'Assises, taking with him no more than a few sandwiches and a small flask of coffee, and there he stayed, fasting, excited, emotionally on edge, till five o'clock at which time he returned to the centre of the city—in a crowd of persons who were not, as he was, in that pleasing condition of men whose lives had been changed as the result of some special stimulus—feeling lonely and melancholy because the excitement was over."[3] But the fictional Jean attends the trial every day; Marcel managed to get there only a few times.

On May 23, 1898, Zola's second libel trial began. Three weeks later he was convicted yet again and sentenced to serve one year in prison and pay a fine, whereupon he fled to London. Events were now moving quickly. Over the course of the summer and into the autumn Jean Jaurès—France's great and tragic Socialist leader, destined to be assassinated in a Montmartre café at the onset of the Great War—published in *La Petite République* his series of unanswerable arguments for the innocence of Dreyfus, quickly collected in book form as *Les Preuves*, by which time Colonel Henry admitted to having forged the *faux Henry*. Arrested and confined at Mont-Valérien fortress, Henry slit his throat on the last day of August. This suicide, in effect a confession, prompted Mme Dreyfus to petition for a full judicial review of her husband's conviction. On September 31, with Marcel somewhere in the throng, Jaurès delivered an electrifying address on the case before the Chamber of Deputies. This firsthand experience of the great orator contributed to Proust's portrait of him as Couzon, the Socialist leader in *Jean Santeuil*. So moved was he by Picquart's plight, powerfully told by Jaurès, that he sought for ways to get a copy of *Pleasures and Days* to the general in prison, which may not have been what Picquart most needed. Marcel had met him, albeit in passing, at one of the evenings that Georges Charpentier, publisher at Calmann-Lévy, organized on behalf of Zola, and was no different from other young authors in believing his book to be an all-purpose blessing.

In the opening pages of *The Captive*, volume five of the *Search*, Proust would dramatize the pitch of hysteria France had come to in those days. Basin de Guermantes inveighs against the treachery of Dreyfus and all his coreligionists: "That shocking crime is not simply a Jewish cause, but *well and truly* an affair of vast national importance which may bring the most appalling consequences for France, which ought to have driven out all the Jews, whereas I'm sorry to say that the sanctions taken up to the present have been directed (in an ignoble fashion, which should be overruled) not against them but against the most eminent of their adversaries, against men of the highest rank who have been cast aside to the ruin of our unhappy country."[4] The most eminent of the Jews' adversaries, here referred to by the Duc de Guermantes, would have been Boisdeffre, Henry, and others of the conspiracy to shield Esterhazy. When forced to acknowledge that conspiracy, anti-Dreyfusards retreated to a new line of argument, calling it noble, self-sacrificing. Charles Maurras, for example, proclaimed the *faux Henry* "a patriotic forgery."

Worth noting also is the extraordinary restaurant scene in part two of *The Guermantes Way* in which Saint-Loup runs gallantly to borrow the Prince de Foix's vicuña cloak when he sees that the Narrator has taken a chill, then scampers back across the tops of the banquettes. We are told, bizarrely, that this restaurant is equipped with a "door reserved for the Hebrews." This leap into the irreal—no restaurant had such a door—ably serves Proust in his rendering of France's folly: "The little group which met to try to grasp and to perpetuate the fugitive emotions aroused by the Zola trial attached a similar importance to this particular café. But they were not viewed with favor by the young nobles who composed the other part of the clientele and had taken over a second room, separated from the other only by a flimsy parapet topped with a row of plants. These looked upon Dreyfus and his supporters as traitors."[5]

Finally, in *Sodom and Gomorrah* there is this: "A considerable period of time had elapsed during which, if, from the historical point of view, events had to some extent seemed to justify the Dreyfusard thesis, the anti-Dreyfusard opposition had greatly increased in violence, and from being purely political had become social. It was now a question of militarism, of patriotism, and the waves of anger that had been stirred up in society had had time to gather the force that they never have at the beginning of a storm. 'Don't you see,' M. de Guermantes went on, 'even from the point of view of his beloved Jews, since he is absolutely determined to stand by them, Swann has made a blunder of incalculable significance. He has proved that they're all secretly united and are somehow forced to give their support to anyone of their own race, even if they don't know him personally. It's a public menace. We've obviously been too easy-going.'"[6]

On September 4, 1898, Esterhazy fled, first to Belgium, then to England, after a nephew revealed evidence of forged telegrams his uncle had sent in the effort to frame Picquart. Esterhazy's delusional account, *Le Dessous de l'Affaire Dreyfus*, appeared at the end of the year. He afterward lived in Hertfordshire under the pseudonym Count Jean de Volmont.

But neither the suicide of Henry nor the flight of Esterhazy put an end to the Dreyfus Affair, which had another year to run, not to speak of its ghoulish afterlife. On November 24, 1898, Picquart's court-martial on baseless charges of forgery and espionage began. Marcel signed a petition in the Colonel's behalf that appeared in *L'Aurore* (though his name, not one to conjure with, was left off till the third time the petition ran).

On June 3, 1899, the Court of Cassation reversed the 1894 verdict against Dreyfus and ordered a new court-martial, this time at Rennes. One day later Zola returned from his months of English exile. Four days after that, Dreyfus began his journey back to France from Devil's Island. On July 1, having arrived at Port-Haligan, he was transferred to Rennes, where the proceedings would include an attempt on the life of Ferdinand Labori, his (as well as Zola's) lawyer, who escaped with a slight wound. Marcel sent Labori a presumptuous telegram praising "the good invincible giant."[7] As for the assailant, he was never identified. On September 9, despite the overwhelming evidence of his innocence, Alfred Dreyfus was reconvicted, though magnanimously spared a second degradation. Ten days later President Émile Loubet offered him a pardon that, despite the implication of guilt, Dreyfus felt compelled to accept.

* * *

Regretting that the Affair had come between them, Proust would write to Pierre d'Orléans, a lieutenant under whom he'd served during his military year, that he wondered why friendships that could weather disagreements about art, morals, even politics, should have foundered on the guilt or innocence of this one man, so categorically had a question of fact, not principle, divided a nation and estranged friend from friend. "If a decorated general is Dreyfusard he immediately becomes despicable to those calling themselves friends of the army, if someone bearing a noble name is Dreyfusard the aristocracy renounce him, if a priest is Dreyfusard the Catholics abuse him. On the other hand, if a civilian is anti-Dreyfusard he acquires from this a military luster; if a radical is anti-Dreyfusard all the priests vote for him; if a Jew is anti-Dreyfusard the anti-semites shield him and the Faubourg Saint-Germain embraces him. And there you have it, pure and simple."[8]

During those Dreyfus-mad months Marcel had traveled briefly and on his own to Amsterdam—it was in September 1898—to view a Rembrandt exhibition, the greatest of its kind up to then, 120 pictures at the newly opened Stedelijkmuseum. The essay he afterward wrote marked an important development of his own aesthetic. The artist, he writes there, is someone more subject to reality than other people, whose work is "in no way a parading of out-of-the-way qualities, but the expression of what had lain nearest to him in his life, and of what lies deepest in things."[9] This piece of writing is particularly significant for containing Proust's first use of the word "translation" as the artist's task. It will gain definitive statement in *Time Regained* when the Narrator says that "the essential, the only true book, though in the ordinary sense it does not have to be 'invented' by a great writer—for it exists already in each one of us—has to be translated by him. The function and the task of a writer are those of a translator."[10]

Still more prophetic for the *Search* is a Christmas letter to Marie Nordlinger, Reynaldo's English cousin—a painter and sculptor—in which there is a first sketch of the involuntary memory theme. Marcel writes of how the recollections of Christmases past "return to us overlaid with the delectable honey of our personality, which we have unconsciously been depositing over the years while—engrossed in selfish pursuits—we paid no attention, and now suddenly it sets our hearts to beating." He is twenty-eight and still nine years from the start of the as-yet-unimagined great work. But already one finds the slowly accreting conviction that *unbidden* memory is the artist's passport to "true impressions," as he'll call them, that these alone "resuscitate the timeless man within me" and are the source of all beauty and all joy.[11]

* * *

Meanwhile, however, he felt disheartened by the lumpy slackness of the Santeuil manuscript, his focus since autumn 1895. Amassing the better part of a thousand pages by 1897, he had added to them in a desultory way till, in 1899, he put the troubled book away.

To come to *Jean Santeuil* after the *Search*—as every student of Proust does—is an eerie experience. One finds so many of the motifs and preoccupations of the later work, but undigested and weakly autobiographical where the *Search* would be colossally inventive. By no means inartistic, it nonetheless feels unorchestrated. People will go on trying to account for this beautiful and distinguished failure. Suffice it to say that the infrared of genius is present there, though visible only to those who know the later work. If his reputation rested on the episodic tale of Jean, Proust's name would be known to only a few specialists. But as Carter writes: "Although deeply discouraged when he abandoned *Jean Santeuil*, Proust had learned more than he realized. He stood closer to his goal than he knew, but was unable to see, in the ruins of his discarded manuscript, the makings of the world the Narrator would inhabit."[12]

Marcel learned of Dreyfus's reconviction while taking the waters at Évian with his parents. He stayed on alone at the Hôtel Splendide that September, absorbed by a book Robert de Billy had lent him, Émile Mâle's *L'Art religieux du XII siècle en France*. In a letter to his mother back in Paris, he asked that along with more cash she send La Sizeranne's *John Ruskin et la religion de l'art*. A great new venture was aborning in him, even as hopes for the novel expired.

Staff at the increasingly empty Spendide were genuinely fond of Marcel, always a munificent tipper. But he stayed on and on, the last remaining guest, to try the patience of employees past due for their next jobs at Nice and other watering places. Still, it is reported that upon the winsome Monsieur Proust's departure, several were in tears.

What was he doing in those weeks? Fretting; dreaming of a trip to the Italian lakes and on from there to Venice. In the event, he returned to Paris on October 8 and, within a few days, was at the Bibliothèque Nationale reading Ruskin excerpts in the various French periodicals. *The Seven Lamps of Architecture* and *The Crown of Wild Olive* were both about to appear in translation. It was at this moment that he definitively abandoned *Santeuil* in order to dedicate himself to Ruskin, setting to work on a study for *La Revue de Paris*. Still more significant, he began to translate, with his mother's help, *The Bible of Amiens*. On December 5 he wrote a particularly revealing letter to Marie Nordlinger: "I have been working for years on a very long-term project, but without getting anywhere. And there are times when I wonder if I do not resemble Dorothea Brooke's husband in *Middlemarch* and if I am not a collector of ruins. For the past fortnight I have been working on a little piece quite different from what I usually write, about Ruskin and certain cathedrals."[13] Marie responded by sending her annotated copy of Ruskin's *The Queen of the Air.* Six weeks later, on January 20, Ruskin died at Brantwood, his Lake District house, following years of silence and mental devastation. Next day Marcel wrote to Marie: "I am shown how paltry a thing death is when I see how vigorously this dead man lives."[14] A week later he published his eulogy in *La Chronique des arts et de la curiosité*, and on February 13 "Ruskin-Inspired Pilgrimages in France" appeared in *Le Figaro.* Marcel was staking a claim as Ruskin's major exponent in France. In April he published "Ruskin at Notre-Dame d'Amiens" in the *Mercure de France.* At Éditions Ollendorff, Paul Ollendorff offered to bring out the translation of *The Bible of Amiens.* Marcel had found the vital way forward.

We have an indeliable portrait at this moment by Léon Daudet, whose *Salons et journaux*, a memoir of youth published in 1917, depicts the young Ruskinite in search of friends at Café Weber—a "pale doe-eyed young man sucking on or fingering the ends of his dark, drooping moustache, and swaddled in layers of wool like a Chinese curio. . . . Soon there fell from his lips, in hesitant bursts, remarks of extraordinary originality, observations of fiendish acuity."[15]

With a view to the upcoming Exposition Universelle, Paris was in 1900 a demon of self-improvement. The new subway system was inaugurated with its exquisite Hector Guimard entryways. The Grand and Petit Palais were completed, along with three new railway stations: Lyon, Orsay, Invalides. The city's most opulent bridge, named for Tsar Alexander III, was opened. The first Michelin *guides verts* were published. On April 15 the immense fair opened for its 212-day run. More than fifty million people flocked to the Champ de Mars, Colline de Chaillot, Esplanade des Invalides, and Place de la Concorde to get a look at what the twentieth century would offer. A moving sidewalk, the Street of the Future, conveyed people from exhibit to exhibit.

In mid-February 1900 Marcel's six-year-long charade of employment at Bibliothèque Mazarine finally ended when, after five years of not showing up for work, the phantom librarian's request for a further leave of absence was rejected. Had he ever done an honest day's work there? One wonders how the pretense lasted as long as it did. At all events, "the only job one cannot be sacked from" would henceforth be the only job Marcel Proust claimed to hold.

Chapter Five

In May 1900, while the world flocked to Paris and its world's fair, Proust left home on the most important journey of his life. Here in *The Captive* the Narrator meditates on the magical name of his and Marcel's destination: "'Venice': a decanted springtime which, reduced to its own essence, expresses the lengthening, the warming, the gradual unfolding of its days in the progressive fermentation, no longer, now, of an impure soil, but of a blue virginal water, spring-like without bud or blossom, which could answer the call of May only by gleaming facets fashioned and polished by May, harmonizing exactly with it in the radiant, unalterable nakedness of its dusky sapphire."[1]

Venice had been his longed-for goal, with an additional reason for the journey—Ruskin—now superadded. Whatever the threat to his health, he had to go "in order to have been able, before dying, to draw close to, to touch and see the em-

Marcel in Venice. Mante-Proust Collection

bodiment of Ruskin's ideas on domestic architecture in the Middle Ages in palaces that are crumbling, but which are still rose-colored and are still standing."[2] Rooms had been reserved for Jeanne and him at the Hôtel de l'Europe (housed then in Palazzo Giustiniani), whose façade was to figure so centrally in the Venetian chapter of *The Fugitive:* "At twelve o'clock each day, when my gondola brought me back for lunch, from afar I often noticed Mama's shawl hung over her alabaster balcony with a book to weigh it down against the wind. And above were the circular foils of her window, lit up like a smile, exuding the reassurance and the confidence that a friendly look imparts. . . . And if I cried the day I saw it again, it was simply because it said to me, 'I remember your mother well.' "[3]

At the railway station to greet them on the morning of their arrival were Marie, her aunt, and Reynaldo, all stopping nearby at Palazzo Fortuny-Madrazo. It was to be a working holiday; Marcel and Marie immediately began to translate *The Bible of Amiens.* She would do literal French versions of Ruskin's sentences; Marcel would then proustify them. In the heat of late afternoon they would explore the city, *The Stones of Venice* and *St. Mark's Rest* serving as guidebooks. Proust would later find exquisite use for memories of gondola rides, gelati at Florian's, whirling flocks of pigeons in Piazza San Marco, and memories of taking shelter in the cathedral baptistery from "those moments of storm and darkness when the mosaics gleamed only with their own material light, with an ancient, internal, terrestrial gold."[4] Most important of all for the *Search* would be a homelier recollection: the uneven paving stones within the baptistery. Uneven paving stones will trigger, in the climactic sequence of *Time Regained*, an involuntary memory of that pavement and bring on the climactic and redemptive revelations at the afternoon party of the Princesse de Guermantes.

Despite worsening asthma—travel always seemed to increase the frequency and severity of his attacks—Marcel managed a side trip to Padua to see Giotto's frescoes in the Arena Chapel and Mantegna's frescoes in the Ovetari Chapel of the Church of the Eremitani (destroyed by Allied bombing in the Second World War).

He and Jeanne were evidently back in Paris by mid-June. On the first day of August "John Ruskin," Proust's most significant essay to date, appeared in the *Gazette des Beaux-Arts*. Here Ruskin's aesthetics have enabled Marcel to crystallize his own: art as new knowledge of nature—escape from the rationalist dichotomy of inner and outer, subjectivity and objectivity, into an intensity of seeing that artist and audience share. One thinks of the episode in *Sodom and Gomorrah* when the Narrator observes on the wall of the drawing room at La Raspelière, the Verdurins' house at the Normandy coast, an early watercolor of roses by Elstir, their ex-friend. The little work stands suddenly for all of art: "Elstir was unable to look at a flower without first transplanting it to that inner garden in which we are obliged always to remain. He had shown in this watercolor the appearance of the roses he had seen, and which, but for him, no one would ever have known."[5] A fresh reality, neither subjective nor objective but artistic, is declared. Elstir's roses gaze back laughingly at the human scene. They are a world elsewhere, vastly more real than La Raspelière and its dinner parties.

Art divinizes, according to Ruskin, according to Proust. Of course the great difference between them was, as Tadié says, that the "Bible lay at the heart of Ruskin's aesthetics; it was his religious fervor that had guided his aesthetic feelings; Proust would retain the divine without the religion."[6] Judaism and Christianity, the enemy creeds of Marcel's maternal and paternal ancestors, had beautifully canceled out in him. He was what he would remain: a congregation of one.

* * *

In October 1900 Marcel made a mysterious second trip to Venice—evidently alone, though Douglas Ainslie may have accompanied him. About this journey nothing can be ascertained. The need to see certain treasures again? The need to see alone, if alone he was, what he'd seen with others on the previous trip? Was it the baptistery in particular? One can only speculate. There were public events, meanwhile, to take note of. In November newspapers briefly reported the death in Paris of Oscar Wilde at a fleabag on rue des Beaux Arts. A month later headlines blazoned the general amnesty for all involved in the Affair, foreclosing any chance of proving at law the guilt of those who'd acted criminally against Dreyfus (now reinstated with the rank of major).

A considerable disorientation that autumn was the Prousts' move to new quarters at 45, rue de Courcelles. On the same street, at 69, lived Princesse Hélène Bibesco with her two sons, Emmanuel and Antoine. The princess was yet another important *salonnière*, hosting Massenet, Debussy, France, Lemaître, Loti, Renan, Leconte de Lisle, Maeterlinck, Bonnard, Redon, Vuillard, and others. Paderewski had made his Paris debut in her drawing room. Her younger son, Antoine, was a Romanian

Foyer 45, Rue de Courcelles. Benjamin Taylor

diplomat whom Marcel had liked on their first encounter at Évian a year earlier. In the course of 1901, liking turned to love. Before long he was speaking recklessly to Antoine about "Salaïsme," the term of the day for homosexuality, coined upon an exceedingly flamboyant Parisian, Count Sala. As usual with young men he wanted, Marcel sailed too near the wind, then had to tack away, reassuring Antoine that inversion interested him only as did, say, Gothic architecture. But early in the new year of 1902 he can be seen to renew the dangerous theme, if censoriously: "I have had some rather profound thoughts about Salaïsm, which will be communicated to you in one of our next metaphysical discussions. There is no need to tell you that they are of extreme severity. Yet as far as people are concerned it remains a philosophical curiosity. Dreyfusard, anti-Dreyfusard,

Salaïst, anti-Salaïst, these are virtually the only things worth knowing about an imbecile."[7] Can he not have understood that he was giving away the game every time he broached the topic? In January, to make matters worse, Marcel sealed with Antoine another of his ill-advised gambits for exclusive attention, this one a pact obliging each to pass along, without fail, what people were saying behind the other's back.

Such contracts were the death knell, and in fact Marcel was already falling in love anew, this time with Vicomte Bertrand de Fénelon—"His Blue Eyes," as he called him, or else "Nonelef," a mysterious anagram. This passion would span, like others, about eighteen months. As nearly all his letters to Bertrand remain in the hands of uncooperative collectors, or else were destroyed by the Fénelon family—aristocrats who regarded Bertrand's connection to such a bourgeois upstart as unsavory—the details cannot be researched. My sense is that the friendship must have included some intimated promise of physical fulfillment, or at least so Marcel interpreted the viscount's behavior. In August, at Restaurant Larue, 15, place de la Madeleine, observing that his friend had taken a chill, Bertrand dashed off, like Saint-Loup in *The Guermantes Way*, to find a coat. Having found one, he rushed back along the banquette around the edge of the wall, leaping over jutting electrical lights as if they were hurdles. The young man with the chill wanted such a gesture to betoken love, not just friendship. Perhaps it did. Only some years later would Marcel learn of Bertrand's "bimétallisme"—slang for bisexuality—much as the Narrator belatedly learns of Saint-Loup's.

* * *

On July 14 Charles Haas, preeminent man about town and familiar of all the best drawing rooms—without achievement beyond his sexual and social triumphs but "superb in intuition, refinement and intelligence," as Boni de Castellane would describe him—died of a cerebral hemorrhage in his apartment on avenue de Villiers. It was an event that went unnoted in Proust's surviving correspondence, not altogether surprisingly. Though afterward the chief key to Charles Swann, Haas was never a man the author of *In Search of Lost Time* knew well. Charles Ephrussi, whom he knew much better, contributed far less to Swann, a fact that prompts this reflection from Tadié: "The case [of Haas] is a curious one and it provides a clue to a kind of law of literary biography: someone who plays a walk-on part in real life may become an important character in a book, because an image, which coincides with one's secret expectations, may resound in the imagination for a long time; in contrast, old friends, brothers, even lovers, may disappear without trace."[8]

At this time a cardiologist named Vaquez prescribed, as a substitute for Veronal, one gram a day of trional for Marcel's erratic pulse. Both these drugs were to become lifelong addictions and would do him grievous harm over the years. On September 30, 1902, he got the news, along with the rest of the world, that the great novelist and hero of the Dreyfus years, Émile Zola, had died in his bedroom of smoke inhalation. Major Dreyfus attended the interment at Montmartre Cemetery, despite threats to his safety. Anatole France delivered the eulogy. (Inevitably, theories that Zola had been murdered quickly sprang up; and have persisted.) One day earlier Marcel had learned that Paul Ollendorff was reneging on his commitment to bring out *La Bible*, whereupon he contacted Alfred Vallette, managing editor at Mercure de France. A long and complicated, ultimately fruitful negotiation to publish began. No contract would be signed until February 1904. As was his wont in such negotiations, Marcel unwisely began by offering to pay the costs. Rich-boy largess would again and again incline him to make this gesture; he was slow to grasp that a book for which the author offers to pay costs is by implication inferior.

On October 3, reading aloud appropriate passages from Fromentin and Taine on the train, he and Bertrand traveled together to Bruges in order to see an exhibition of Flemish art. Then on to Dordrecht, where Marcel climbed the tower of the Grote Kerk. Then by boat to Rotterdam. After that, Antwerp and on to the Hôtel de l'Europe at Amsterdam. Then, on his own, Marcel took the tramway to Monniendam and a boat to Volendam. On October 17 he was in Haarlem to view the Halses, and the next day in The Hague, where, at the Mauritsuis Royal House, he saw what was to be the most important painting in the *Search*—Vermeer's *View of Delft:* "the most beautiful painting in the world," he pronounced it. At Delft he noted "the innocent waters of the canal which a little pale sunlight causes to glitter between the double rows of trees, leafless since the end of summer, and to shimmer in the mirrors that are hung outside the gabled houses on either bank."[9]

All these travels may be placed under the sign of his love for Bertrand. Marcel felt more vividly alive, and knew the brevity of what he was feeling, inasmuch as the beloved was scheduled to take up diplomatic duties in Constantinople by the third week of December. With the date of departure approaching, Marcel was increasingly nervous. The following wild episode of temper, which will furnish inspiration for the great hat-stomping scene in *The Guermantes Way*, is known to us from an in-house letter to his mother, reproaching her for allowing the servants to make noise after he'd taken his trional and was attempting to sleep: "Thanks to you, I was in such a state of nerves that when poor Fénelon came with Lauris, because of something he said—extremely unpleasant I have to say—I flew at him with my fists (Fénelon, not Lauris), and not knowing what I was doing, I seized the new hat he had just bought, trampled on it, tore it to pieces and then ripped out the lining. As you probably think I'm exaggerating, I enclose a piece of the lining so that you can see I'm telling the truth."[10]

On December 18 a more composed Marcel was at Gare de Lyon to see Bertrand off on the Orient Express.

* * *

Two days after that, in a letter to Antoine, he made the startling confession that Ruskin had begun to bore him: "It's enough to awaken my thirst for achievement, without in any way assuaging it. Now that for the first time since my long torpor I have looked at myself and my thoughts introspectively, I can sense all the insignificance of my life; hundreds of characters for novels, a thousand ideas urging me to give them substance. . . . My intelligence was enslaved by my need for peace of mind. In throwing off its chains, I thought I was merely freeing a slave, but I was giving myself a master."[11] This important year-end confession marks a new stage in self-understanding. Which is not to suggest he'd become less proprietary about Ruskin; or less touchy about his uncertain grasp of English. In an irate letter to Constantin de Bracovan, editor in chief of *La Renaissance Latine*, where excerpts from *La Bible* were scheduled to appear, he declared: "I don't claim to know English. I claim to know Ruskin."[12] But as Richard Macksey has said, a great deal of time and energy were being expended on a figure who ultimately was not Marcel's type, and he'd begun to know it.[13]

On February 2, 1903, at thirty-two, he served as best man in his brother's wedding. The scene was outlandish. Marcel arrived stuffed with thermal wadding inside a cutaway over which he wore several overcoats against the winter chill of Église Saint-Augustin. A young cousin, Valentine Thomson, would recall the "Lazarus-like countenance, with its melancholy moustache pushed up rather comically by his black woolen cerements. He felt he had to explain himself, and at every pew in turn, he announced in a loud voice that he was unable to dress in any other way, that he had been ill for months, that he would be still more ill that evening, and that it was not his fault."[14]

Three weeks later, under the pseudonym Dominique, Marcel published "The Historic Salon of Princess Mathilde," the first of what would be his series in *Le Figaro* on notable Paris *salons* and *salonnières*. But as his social life grew more and more brilliant, the outlook for love was darkening. All doors of fashionable society swung wide; no social conquest was beyond his charms. Yet reciprocated love—that seemed an impossible goal. The latest crush, the Marquis Louis d'Albufera, was entirely heterosexual and out of reach. In a letter to Madame de Pierrebourg, Marcel wrote: "I know that shared love between people exists. But alas, I do not know their secret."[15]

In addition to the "Salons" coming out pseudonymously, there seem to have been two quick jobs of ghostwriting. It was likely Marcel who composed the address his father delivered in July at Chartres to inaugurate the statue of Louis Pasteur in Place Saint-Michel, and it was very likely Marcel who wrote Dr. Proust's prize-day speech at Illiers, where he conjures a landscape all but ready to become sempiternal Combray: "Today it is among those wide spaces whose power lies in their monotony that the landscape painter will most willingly go in search of his innermost feelings among these interminable wheat fields which, like the sea, alter according to the whims of sunbeam and shadow, breeze and swell."[16] The bluff and matter-of-fact Dr. Proust did not write that; it is in the unmistakable voice of his elder son.

Sometime in July or August Marcel managed to lose, somewhere in his anarchic bedroom, the page proofs of *La Bible* that Mercure de France had set in type. In despair he forsook the Ruskin project, on which he had labored for four years. This must have seemed more than a little theatrical. The proofs had to be somewhere in that mess. Instead of looking harder he joined his parents on their August holiday at the Grand Hôtel Victoria, Interlaken, with its famous view of the Jungfrau. From there he went alone to Avallon. Unable to sleep on the overnight train, Marcel saw his first sunrise in many years, which in a letter to Georges de Lauris he declared preferable to sunset. After touring the monuments of Avallon on foot, he hired a car to Vézelay, superbly described in the same letter: "A fantastic place, in a sort of Switzerland, all alone on top of a mountain that towers above all others, visible on all sides for miles around and set among the most strikingly harmonious scenery. The church is vast and looks as much like a Turkish bath as it does Notre-Dame, built in alternating blocks of black and white stone, a lovely Christian mosque."[17] On to Dijon to see the tombs of Philip the Bold and his kin at the Palace of the Dukes. Marcel, the worse for wear and running a fever, rejoined his parents, now at the Splendide, Évian, where he remained till October 10.

Meanwhile in Paris *Le Figaro* published "Salon of the Princess of Polignac," another in the series of "Dominique" pieces. In mid-October Marcel's route home, in the company of Louisa de Mornand and Louis d'Alfubera, included a visit to Chamonix, loved by Ruskin, and an arduous climb up Montanvert to stroll on its frozen sea. Despite weakness and vulnerability to asthma, Marcel had become, under Ruskin's guidance, an unstoppable sightseer. Before October was out he'd made his way to Brou for the flamboyant Gothic church and to Beaune to visit the Hospices.

* * *

"The great prolonged feast of life," Carter writes, "was ending for his father's generation, whose youth had known the best days of the Second Empire."[18] On November 24 Adrien suffered a cerebral hemorrhage while teaching and was brought home on a stretcher. The following day Marthe, Robert's wife, gave birth to Suzanne-Adrienne Proust—"Adrienne" in honor of the stricken father. On November 26, at 9 A.M., after a life rich in achievement, Adrien Proust died in the presence of his wife and sons. He was not quite seventy. Following the service on November 28 at Église Saint-Philippe-du-Roule, he was conveyed with military escort to the cemetery of Père-Lachaise.

In the first weeks of grieving, Marcel wrote to Anna de Noailles: “I am well aware that I was always the dark spot in his life.”[19] And ten months later, in a letter to his mother: “One has to work out the dates in order to be able to tell oneself that already ten months have gone by, that one has already been unhappy for such a long time, that one would continue to be so for a long time to come, and that for the past ten months poor little Papa had no longer enjoyed anything and no longer knew the sweetness of life.”[20]

Chapter Six

At the turn of 1903, armed with fresh page proofs from Mercure de France, Marcel made the final pass at his translation of *The Bible of Amiens.* It was published on February 27 and dedicated "to the memory of my father, struck down at work." The dedicatory page included also a portion of the following from Ruskin's *Fors Clavigera:* "Youth is properly the forming time—that in which a man makes himself, or is made, what he is for ever to be. Then comes the time of labour, when having become the best he can be, he does the best he can do. Then the time of death, which in happy lives is very short."

Maurice Barrès wrote a congratulatory letter about the *Bible* and suggested that Marcel turn next to Walter Pater. But Marcel knew he hadn't the luxury of again playing disciple. "I shall certainly not be the one who translates him," he responded. "I still have two Ruskins to do, and after that I shall try to translate my own poor soul, if it doesn't die in the meantime."[1] France's major philosopher, Henri Bergson, praised him for introducing Ruskin to French readers, and the leading historian of the day, Albert Sorel, wrote a favorable review in *Le Temps.* Here was recognition of a kind Proust had not known with *Pleasures and Days.*

In April Marie Nordlinger sent a present of dried Japanese flowers that unfold in water. These would furnish Proust, in the prelude to *Swann's Way,* with his most famous simile: Involuntary memory, triggered by a taste of madeleine dipped in lime-blossom tea, causes the lost world of Combray to rise up "as in the game wherein the Japanese amuse themselves by filling a porcelain bowl with water and steeping in it little pieces of paper which until then are without character or form, but, the moment they become wet, stretch and twist and take on colour and distinctive shape, become flowers or houses or people, solid and recognizable, so in that moment all the flowers in our garden and in M. Swann's park, and the water-lilies on the Vivonne and the good folk of the village and their little dwellings and the parish church and the whole of Combray and its surroundings, taking shape and solidity, sprang into being, town and gardens alike, from my cup of tea."[2]

By now nocturnal as any bat or possum, he did manage, on June 7, 1904, a daylight outing to the Durand-Ruel Gallery in order to see thirty-nine canvases by Monet (and took in, as well, Walter Sickert's views of Venice and Dieppe at the Bernheim-Jeaune). But nearly all of Marcel's public appearances these days were after nightfall, at the *salons* and aristocratic parties. In a letter to Antoine Bibesco he quotes Ruskin to the effect that his gadding about in fashionable society is only "the apparent life," whereas "the real life is underneath all this"[3]—a presaging of what will be the central insight of *Contre Sainte-Beuve* (1908–9), the unpublished manuscript that would modulate into *Le Temps Perdu,* Proust's first draft of the *Search:* "A book is the product of a different self from the one we mani-

Église Saint-Jacques, Illiers. Nicolas Drogoul

fest in our habits, in society, in our vices. If we mean to try to understand this self it is only in our inmost depths, by endeavoring to reconstruct it there, that the quest can be achieved."[4]

In August he made one of the last journeys of his life, cruising the Brittany coast on Robert de Billy's father's yacht, the *Hélène*. A blurry photo of Marcel on deck with other guests survives. But yachting did not agree with him; he debarked at Dinard and went home to Paris. His health was becoming too precarious for trips of any kind. On November 25, one day before the anniversary of Dr. Proust's death, he toiled up to Père-Lachaise bearing flowers and came home with a wracking cold. Still convalescent, he received from his mother, as a New Year's Day gift, the published portion of the Library Edition of Ruskin's work, which would appear six volumes at a time between 1903 and 1912. Meanwhile mother and son continued their Ruskin labors. On March 1 "On the Treasures of the Kings," the first lecture from *Sesame and Lilies*, appeared in *Les Arts de la vie;* two more installments followed on April 15 and May 15. These were finer renderings than those of *The Bible*. Proust had made good on the old boast: Whatever his independent grasp of English, he and Jeanne between them now knew Ruskin faultlessly.

But something more fundamental was under way. He was gaining, by a slow but inexorable process, the skills that would carry him far beyond *Jean Santeuil* and the Ruskin translations and set him on the path of the *Search*. "At the end," he was shortly to write in "On Reading," his preface to the translation of Ruskin's *Sesame and Lilies*, "one has followed some kind of secret plan that, when it is finally revealed, imposes a retrospective order on the whole work and makes it appear to lead, in a series of magnificent steps, to that final apotheosis."[5] This hauntingly foretells the great work to come, as if Proust were glimpsing a continent as yet unnamed.

On the night of June 24 he didn't go to bed at all in order to attend a morning *vernissage* of 440 paintings, engravings, and lithographs by James Abbott McNeill Whistler—Ruskin's mortal enemy but a great admiration of Marcel's—at the École des Beaux-Arts. And had the expectable asthma attack afterward. Even without the prospect of 440 Whistlers, Marcel might have had trouble sleeping; it was on this same day that "On Reading" was to appear in *La Renaissance Latine*. He surely knew this to be his most significant piece of writing so far. "Mediocre people generally believe that to let oneself be guided by books one admires takes away some of one's independence of judgment," whereas the best people "feel that their power to understand and feel is infinitely increased" by contact with greatness. "We are then simply in a state of grace in which all our faculties, our critical sense as well as our other senses, are strengthened. Therefore, this voluntary servitude . . . is the beginning of freedom. There is no better way of trying to recreate in oneself what a master has felt." The critic or man of letters develops into a sovereign artist by first indenturing himself; and discovers freedom through subordination.

At the conclusion of "On Reading" Proust's mature theme shimmers into view. Evoking the Piazzeta at Venice, he writes: "Around the pink columns, surging up toward their wide capitals, the days of the present crowd and buzz. But, interposed between them, the columns push them aside, reserving with all their slender impenetrability the inviolate place of the Past: of the Past familiarly risen in the midst of the present, with that rather unreal complexion of things which a kind of illusion makes us see a few steps ahead, and which are actually situated back many centuries; appealing in its whole aspect a little too positively to the mind, overexciting it a little, as should not be surprising on the part of a ghost from a buried past; yet there, in our midst, approached, pressed against, touched, motionless, in the sun."

It is no exaggeration to say that "On Reading" is the germ of everything that follows. A farewell to Ruskin, it declares the author's independence for the primary—never again secondary—work to come. Writing in May to Albert Sorel, his admirer and former teacher, he says that illness has more and more compelled him "to do without nearly everything and to replace people by their images and life by thought."[6] But it was not only, or even primarily, asthma that was working the change. Imagination had begun catalyzing experience in a new way, granting the means by which to reclaim life's losses.

* * *

In *The Guermantes Way* Proust writes: "We may, indeed, say that the hour of death is uncertain; but when we say this we think of that hour as situated in a vague and remote expanse of time; it does not occur to us that it can have any connection with the day that has already dawned and can mean that death—or its first assault and personal possession of us, after which it will never leave hold of us again—may occur this very afternoon, whose timetable, hour by hour, has been settled in advance."[7] On September 6 Marcel accompanied his mother to Évian, where they planned to join Mme Cautusse, her great friend. They'd scarcely checked in at the Splendide when Jeanne suffered an acute attack of nephritis. It was death's opening assault. Perhaps realizing the truth, she called for a photographer, wanting a last image of herself for Marcel, but then was too ill to face the camera. Upon their quick return to Paris she stopped eating and refused all medication, knowing herself in the final stage of kidney failure, the family disease.

On September 24, at eleven o'clock in the morning, Jeanne Weil Proust died. Next day Marcel wrote to Anna de Noailles: "Death restored to her the youthfulness of the day before her sorrows; she hadn't a single white hair. She takes away my life with her, as Papa had taken away hers." Because she had not renounced "her Jewish religion on marrying Papa, because she regarded it as a token of respect for her parents, there will be no church, simply the house tomorrow, Thursday, at 12 o'clock

Marcel, Jeanne, Robert. Bibliothèque Nationale de France,
Dist. RMN-Grand Palais/Art Resource, NY

. . . and the cemetery. . . . Today I have her yet, dead but still receiving my caresses. And then I shall never have her again. . . . I went into certain rooms in the apartment that I had not been back to and explored unknown regions of my grief, which increases endlessly the more it continues. There is a certain floorboard near Maman's bedroom which one cannot walk over without it making a noise, and Maman, the moment she heard it, used to make a little sound with her mouth which meant: Come and give me a kiss."[8] Reynaldo, who'd hurried to his friend's side, would afterward recall Marcel smiling through tears as he watched her in death.

Jeanne Proust was interred at Père-Lachaise by Dr. Proust's side. "Our entire life together," Marcel wrote to Barrès, "was only a period of training for the day when she would leave me, and this has been going on since my childhood when she would refuse to come back ten times and tell me good night before going out for the evening."[9] Years later he said to Céleste Albaret: "You can't imagine how she spoiled us, Céleste, and how solicitous she was. Nothing was ever too good for Robert and me." She would have Félicie, their cook, bake potatoes in their jackets for the boys to use as hand warmers. "I loved my father very much. But on the day Mother died, she took her little Marcel with her."[10]

Among the strangest aspects of *In Search of Lost Time* is that the parents of the Narrator do not die or even grow old in the course of a book spanning decades. Or if they do their decline and their deaths are passed over in silence; but that would make no sort of dramatic sense. It seems rather that they are eventually somewhere outside the frame of the tale, hale and hearty, indeed deathless. In what other multigenerational novel is this the case? Are the parents of Dorothea Brooke in *Middlemarch*, Pierre Besukhov in *War and Peace*, or Thomas Buddenbrook in *Buddenbrooks* exempted from the universal debt? Of course not. But in Proust there is little dying altogether, especially when you consider that it is so much longer than these others. Having dramatized the death of the grandmother in *The Guermantes Way*, he'll dramatize that of Bergotte in *The Captive* and will then have had enough of dying. Here one can offer only speculations and my own is as follows: It was not that Proust wanted to spare his hero, fearing that the Narrator could not bear the loss of his parents. Proust feared that he himself would not survive the writing of such scenes.

By December he had checked into Dr. Paul Sollier's clinic for nervous disorders at 145, rue de Versailles, Boulogne-sur-Seine. He was still there when on January 11 he learned, with utter indifference, that he and his brother had each inherited from their mother twenty-three million francs (about $5 million in American currency in 2015). Maurice Duplay reports in his memoir *Mon Ami Marcel Proust* that Marcel told him he'd resolved to kill himself after Jeanne's death, refraining only because he did not want to appear in the newspapers as a suicide. He had considered starving himself to death as an alternative, but rejected that too when he realized that the vast store of his memories of Jeanne would perish with him.[11]

By the end of January Marcel felt strong enough to return from Dr. Sollier's sanitarium to rue de Courcelles and the apartment where every item spoke of all he'd lost. A curious document of this moment is yet another letter addressed to Barrès—a man who could never bring himself to like Marcel Proust—in order to congratulate him on his election to the Académie Française. Did Proust already dream of standing one day among the *Immortels*, with whose newest member he was seeking to ingratiate himself? "Joyfulness, enthusiasm, for the artist as for the reader, is the criterion of beauty, of genius, of truth,"[12] he wrote by way of congratulation—words presumably shrugged off by their dour and haughty recipient. The whole letter, beneath its obsequious *politesse*, is a deadly accurate assessment of how far short Barrès falls. Proust was measuring himself against a famous writer and finding the famous writer wanting. This seems highly significant so soon after the return from Dr. Sollier's. Some new mettle had sprung from the grief.

André Beaunier reviewed *Sésame et les Lys* favorably in the *Figaro* on June 5, 1906, calling Proust "one of our subtlest and most delicate writers" on the strength of "On Reading," now *Sésame*'s introduction. It was to be a commercial as well as a critical success, going into a fourth printing before the end of the year.

A month later the Affair reached its official conclusion when the Chambre des Députés pronounced Captain—now Major—Dreyfus innocent, an event Proust found ridiculous inasmuch as Dreyfus had always been innocent. On July 21, at the École militaire, in the courtyard where he'd been degraded eleven years earlier, Major Dreyfus received the cross of the Chevalier de la Légion d'honneur. Picquart was also reinstated and promoted.

For his health, and perhaps finding the apartment an unbearable reminder, Marcel left 45, rue de Courcelles and took up residence in Versailles at the Hôtel des Reservoirs (once a property of Mme de Pompadour) for a five-month stay. The news of another death would quickly follow: Uncle Georges Weil, Jeanne's beloved brother, had died of uremia like his sister. While at Versailles Proust decided to abandon rue de Courcelles in favor of what had been his great Uncle Louis's apartment—"the ugliest thing I've ever seen," he called it in a letter to Mme Catusse—at 102, Boulevard Haussmann, a noisy, dusty street then as now, whose only virtue seems to have been that it was not rue de Courcelles.

"I've spent four months in Versailles as though in a telephone kiosk, without being the least aware of my surroundings," he added in the letter to Mme Catusse.[13] At des Reservoirs Marcel sounded the depths of his grief, and wondered whether he'd find strength to work again. "I've closed forever the era of translations," he wrote to Marie Nordlinger, "which Maman encouraged. And as for translations of myself, I no longer have the heart."[14] But this despair was in fact the birthing of an unimaginable new vigor. On a visit to Versailles Reynaldo had given him *Le Chevalier d'Harmental* by Dumas and Marquet, a novel in which part of the action takes place in "rue du Temps-Perdu," Street of Lost (or Wasted) Time. Suddenly the phrase meant something; or rather, everything; and stuck.

It was a ravaged thirty-five-year-old who two days after Christmas installed himself in boulevard Haussmann. But the four walls of a soon-to-be-cork-lined bedroom are going to witness feats of unimaginable vitality—Marcel Proust's transmutation of talent into genius. Now the conscientious man of letters steps aside for the most extraordinary redeemer of lost or wasted time that literature has ever known.

Chapter Seven

On April 27, 1907, Maximilian Harden, editor of Berlin's leading social-democratic weekly, *Die Zukunft*, exposed Philip, Prince of Eulenberg—Kaiser Wilhelm II's best friend, his nearest adviser, and the chief moderating force in his circle—and General Kuno Graf von Moltke as homosexual lovers, precipitating a crisis around the emperor. A series of libel cases resulted, closely followed by Proust for the rest of the year and into 1908. Vigorous attention was paid in France, where "Parlez-vous allemand?" became a homosexual password. In *The Guermantes Way* Charlus, evidently in the know years before the scandal broke, says to our baffled Narrator: "There exists among certain men a freemasonry of which I cannot now say more than that it numbers in its ranks four of the reigning sovereigns of Europe. Now, the entourage of one of these, who is the Emperor of Germany, is trying to cure him of his fancy. That is a very serious matter, and may lead us to war. Yes, my dear sir, that is a fact. You remember the story of the man who believed that he had the Princess of China shut up in a bottle. It was a form of insanity. He was cured of it. But as soon as he ceased to be mad he became merely stupid. There are maladies which we must not seek to cure because they alone protect us from others that are more serious."[1] Deprived of the moderating counsel of von Eulenberg, the kaiser indeed grew excessively stupid. His militaristic goading of Austria in the July Crisis of 1914 would be among the causes of the Great War.

On August 5 Proust departed for Cabourg, establishing a pattern that was to last till 1914. He checked into the newly opened Grand Hôtel, associated to this day with his name. There he came to know Sem, the noted caricaturist, and Paul Helleu, a painter on whom aspects of Elstir (for example, his happy marriage) would be based in the *Search*. A great friend of Sargent and Blanche—and follower of Whistler and Tissot—Helleu was to find his major biographer in none other than Robert de Montesquiou. In 1912 he would travel to New York to design the zodiac ceiling of Grand Central Terminal (painted over in the 1930s but rediscovered and restored in 1998).

For an outing one afternoon to Caen, Proust hired from Taximètres Unic, an operation his old chum Jacques Bizet had founded, a young man from Monaco named Alfred Agostinelli, round and appealing and with a streak of bravado at the wheel of his red cab. The Normandy-coast social season was in full spate and Proust made frequent use of this new driver. Together he and Georges de Lauris paid calls on Mme Straus at Clos des Mûriers, her retreat in Trouville, on the Guiches nearby at their house, Les Rêves, and on Georges's father at Houlgate. As well, Proust visited the great painter Édouard Vuillard at Amfreville—"no ordinary man, even if he does say 'guy' [*type*] every twenty seconds."[2] In *In the Shadow of Young Girls in Flower* Elstir will say, of the "guy" who sculpted the narthex of Balbec church, that he was as good or better than any living artist. Thus a fragment of the man Vuillard passed into Elstir.

On the way back to Paris Proust and Agostinelli halted at Évreux for a look at Nôtre-Dame, its greatly admired cathedral. (No excursion to nearby Giverny; Monet and Proust would never meet.) All this motoring around in Agostinelli's *taxi rouge* would bear literary fruit. On November 9 Proust published "Impressions While Traveling in an Automobile" in the *Figaro:* "My mechanic was clad in a huge rubber mantle and wore a sort of hood fitted tightly round his youthful beardless face and which, as we sped faster and faster into the night, made him look like some pilgrim, or rather, a speed-loving nun."[3] Chauffeurs were still called "mechanics" at the time. This particular mechanic, of scant interest in 1907, will in years to come consume Marcel's emotions and determine the course of his masterwork. Proust will discover—like Swann, like the Narrator—that looking with new eyes at a familiar someone may bring on the cyclone of love.

"On Reading" and "Impressions While Traveling in an Automobile" together reveal, as nothing before them, the mature idiom: relaxed, loose-limbed, light in the halter, intimating profundities with new élan. After long years of application to his native language, and nine of servitude to Ruskin's, Proust at thirty-six had forged the weapon of a style.

* * *

On New Year's Day, 1908, Mme Straus presented Marcel with five long, narrow, decorative notebooks from Kirby Beard, a chic stationer located behind the Opéra. In the largest of these—now called the *carnet de 1908*—Marcel began making notes for what he sometimes called "my Parisian novel." The seventy-five draft pages from these months are lost, unfortunately. He seems to have used the little notebook (it contains about four years' worth of entries) as a digest or inventory and scholars have drawn from it their conclusions about his earliest approach to the *Search*.

Meanwhile an earlier Marcel was coexisting—or rather, finishing his run—alongside this newborn Proust of the momentous *carnet*. On February 22 the *Figaro* ran his pastiches of Balzac, Michelet, the Goncourts, and Faguet, and on March 14 and 22 those of Flaubert, Sainte-Beuve, and Renan. All of these are mock responses by great writers of the past to contemporary news items, particularly one Henri Leomoine's claim that he could manufacture diamonds in a kiln; many investors, including Marcel Proust, had been swindled.

Such trifles were good enough fun but Proust's gorge rose as he wrote them. "No more pastiches," he finally declared to Robert Dreyfus. "What an idiotic exercise."[4] "I am about to embark on a very important piece of work,"[5] he confided to Louis d'Albufera in April and he added that he was planning—presumably in the interest of this new work—to leave Paris forever. Harmless fantasy. Marcel's dreams of a life in Florence or the south of France will remain under the rubric *nom de pays: le nom*—places imagined but unattained.

On May 5 or 6 a significant letter to Albufera enumerated eight ideas for projects: a study of the nobility, a Parisian novel, an essay on Sainte-Beuve and Flaubert, an essay on women, an essay on pederasty (difficult to publish, he noted), and a few more: on Gothic windows, on carved tombs, and on the novel as an art form. Proust will not be long in grasping that these were not discrete undertakings but the themes of one great book. That second item on the list, the "roman parisien," will shortly swell to contain all the others. The realization that he needn't choose among impulses, that inclusiveness was the way forward, became Proust's vitalizing discovery.

* * *

Zola's remains were brought from Cimetière Montmartre to the Panthéon on June 4, 1908, and placed in the crypt alongside France's other national heroes: *pathéonisation*, as it is called. Dreyfus, prematurely aged from his long ordeal on Devil's Island, was in attendance. Following the ceremony a right-wing journalist named Louis A. Gregori stepped from the crowd and fired on the major, wounding him slightly. Gregori was promptly acquitted on grounds that his crime had been one of passion.

Though Marcel's social rounds were more vigorous than ever, his wardrobe was less and less suitable to the smart world he frequented. Boulevard playwright Henri Bernstein had gone around saying that Marcel Proust was too shabby to be seen with at a whorehouse. Stung, he ordered several new suits from Carnaval de Venise, a haberdasher in the neighborhood.

His social business by now had a purpose. Formerly he'd come to be part of the scene. Now he was there to X-ray it. On June 12 he attended a party at the Princesse de Polignac's. His commentary to Mme de Caraman-Chimay would include this: "so many comical faces making an incomparably grotesque frieze."[6] Already the finale of the *Search*, Proust's *bal des têtes*—the famed afternoon *chez* Guermantes, likened to a masquerade at which decrepitude furnishes the disguises—had begun to gestate. On June 22 he attended Princesse Marie Murat's annual summer ball, where he met Mlle Oriane de Goyon, whose Christian name he will make immortal in the figure of Oriane, Duchesse de Guermantes. An encyclopedic gathering-in of the usable data—names dropped, poses struck, backs bitten, plumage worn—was now under way. Proust's insatiable and eidetic memory had begun storing up "what seemed to others puerile trivialities, the tone of voice in which a certain remark had been made, or the facial expression and the movement of the shoulders he had seen at a certain moment, many years ago, in somebody of whom he knows nothing else whatsoever, simply because this tone of voice was one that he had heard before or felt that he might hear again, because it was something renewable, durable."[7]

People who pose for portrait painters know that they are doing so. But novelists work by pocketing bits and pieces of individuals without their consent. Thieves of actuality, they make perpetual what otherwise would vanish. To conduct such thieveries was now Proust's reason for venturing out. Tadié goes farther, arguing that henceforth he provoked new social experiences in order to remember them and that "his life now became his laboratory; memories were no longer enough, and so, like a scientist, he induced experience and invented reality in order to transform these into language."[8] The erstwhile ingénue of the *beau monde* had become a spy and conductor of experiments in its ranks.

If the pose of the toff offered one cover, the pose of the heterosexual offered another. Marcel wrote to Robert Dreyfus: "Do you know (I believe you do) Mme Philippe *née* Fava? I saw her once at Cabourg and not since. But suddenly I feel just a little bit in love with her. Only just a little bit. I seem to recall that she had dark skin and soft eyes."[9] Was this fandango as transparent to Marcel's friends as to us? Men who were themselves homosexual would of course have recognized the pretense. As for the rest, harder to say.

He departed on July 18 for his customary sojourn at Cabourg, from where he wrote to Robert de Billy that "a few Jewish dry-goods merchants make up the hotel's aristocracy; moreover, haughty."[10] While visiting the Gagnats at Chalet Suisse in Bénerville he met Gaston Gallimard, who at this stage scarcely acknowledged the strange and sickly fellow who would one day be his firm's most important author. It was also on this visit that a painful piece of homosexual comic opera—later very useful—took place. In the hotel casino he was introduced to one of the flowering youths who'd caught his eye that year, a nineteen-year-old named Marcel Plantevignes. Young Plantevignes formed the habit of visiting the older man's room every evening for long talks. But when a woman on the boardwalk intimated to the boy that he might be keeping company with an invert, Plantevignes failed to defend Proust, accepting in silence the woman's insinuations. Word of this got back to Proust and he flew into a Charlus-like rage, accusing the young man of stabbing him in the back—"You have carelessly spoiled what could have been a beautiful friendship!"[11]—and challenged the boy's father to a duel for having taken up the slander. Then, as suddenly, he restored cordial relations with the whole family.

"He that loveth well chastiseth well,"[12] Palamède de Charlus says of God and himself. Those content to see Robert de Montesquiou as the model for the baron have neglected an original nearer to home. It is said that when asked on whom she had modeled Edward Casaubon in *Middlemarch*, George Eliot closed her eyes and put a finger to her breast. While Proust would never have admitted to basing Charlus's ill-fated courtship of the Narrator on his own wooing of Marcel Plantevignes, he clearly did so.[13]

* * *

In October or November Proust wrote in the Kirby Beard notebook: "Must I make of it a novel, a philosophical study, am I a novelist?"[14] Near the end of the year he purchased a large number of *cahiers d'écolier*, composition books like those from Condorcet days. Within the next ten or so months—working steadily and with new purpose throughout 1909, Proust's *annus mirabilis*—he filled ten of them, seven hundred pages, with the prose we know under the heading *Contre Sainte-Beuve*. (By his death in 1922 Proust had filled 127 such *cahiers*, 95 of which are conserved at the Bibliothèque Nationale.) A change in energy, drive, focus, and self-confidence is evident. As Tadié says, "In November 1908, a crucial date, Proust began to write Sainte-Beuve and thereafter he did not stop."[15]

In December he put this question in the *carnet:* Was the Sainte-Beuve material to be an essay or a conversation with his mother? Clearly Proust felt himself at a crossroads between discursive and imaginative writing. "May I ask your advice?" he wrote to his friend Georges de Lauris. "I am going to write something about Sainte-Beuve. I have more or less two articles in my head (magazine articles). One is an article that takes the classic form, like an essay by Taine, only less good. The other starts with the description of a morning in which Maman would come to my bedside and I would tell her about the article I want to write on Sainte-Beuve. And I would elaborate on it to her. Which do you reckon is best?"[16]

He of course wanted Lauris to encourage the latter, inherently more interesting and original than a Taine-inspired magazine piece; but the (lost) letter from Lauris seems to have inclined to the essay; and Marcel's next letter to him indicates a disinclination to follow the counsel offered. It was anyhow the advice he gave himself that was now most authoritative: "Perhaps I should bless my ill health, which through sacrifice of tiredness, immobility and silence, has taught me the possibility of working. The intimations of death. Soon you won't be able to say all this. Laziness, doubt or impotence sheltering uncertainty in the guise of art."[17] Tadié writes: "A novel about Sainte-Beuve would be an original and audacious undertaking, because it would be part autobiography—the presence of his mother—and part theory"[18]—autobiography and theory (whatever that big word signifies here) each acting on the other to produce something new that is neither. The gods of fiction have summoned Marcel. He has refined himself to a single purpose. What he writes about Alfred de Musset in the *carnet* is self-portraiture: "In his life and in his letters, just as in a seam of ore in which they are barely recognizable, we glimpse certain lineaments of his work, which was his life's only *purpose* —as well as his loves, which existed only in so far as they were raw material for his work, directed toward work alone and having their only existence in it."[19]

At about this time Proust took the manuscript of *Jean San-*

teuil from the closet where it had lain for nearly a decade and recopied many passages.

It is interesting to catalogue the things from *Santeuil* not reprised in the *Search*. For example the whole experience of school—Jean studies first at Lycée Henri IV and then at École des Sciences Politiques—will disappear. While the Narrator must have had a formal education, there is barely a word about it in the *Search*, a Bildungsroman of a million and a half words. And then there are the elements from *Santeuil* that do recur in the *Search*, always very differently. Let one example suffice: In *Jean Santeuil* the Dreyfus Affair is a matter for courtroom reportage; in the *Search* it is much more profoundly revealed as a contagion laying waste the whole of a society.

* * *

On March 9, 1909, *Le Figaro* ran "The Lemoine Affaire of Henri de Régnier," Proust's last pastiche (until the great one at the outset of *Time Regained*). He then proposed the pastiches as a volume. How little esteemed he was at this time is evident from the rejections fired off by Mercure de France, Calmann-Lévy, and Fasquelle. What he had to offer seemed out of tune with the times. Popular taste lately favored Romain Rolland's *Jean-Christophe*, the ten volumes of which would appear between 1904 and 1912. Proust had sampled and loathed it; indeed, he contemplated writing a "Contre Romain Rolland." It was Diaghilev's Ballets Russes, rather than any new book, that would deeply stir him. In June 1909 they had taken Paris by storm. So powerful is Diaghilev's triumph in the *Search* that the old Dreyfus passions are forgotten, balletomania taking their place. Mme Verdurin has maneuvered herself into the big middle of things, as always: "This charming invasion, against whose seductions only the stupidest of critics protested, infected Paris, as we know, with a fever of curiosity less agonizing, more purely aesthetic, but quite as intense perhaps as that aroused by the Dreyfus case. There too Mme Verdurin, but with a very different result socially, was to be in the vanguard. Just as she had been seen by the side of Mme Zola, immediately below the judge's bench during the trial in the Assize Court, so when the new generation, in their enthusiasm for the Russian ballet, thronged to the Opéra, they invariably saw in a stage box Mme Verdurin, crowned with fantastic aigrettes."[20]

* * *

Marcel had meanwhile been a reckless steward of his large inheritance, speculating in stocks he liked the names of: Tanganyika Railway, Pins des Landes, Australian Gold Mines, Rio Tinto, Tramways de Mexico. When Lionel Hauser, his theosophist financial adviser (sound in money judgment despite vaporous religious views), warned that he would not act as agent for such long-shot investments, Marcel simply sneaked off to other brokers.

In May he questioned Lauris about a name—Guermantes—and "whether it is entirely extinct and available to an author." On July 7, 1909, he wrote to Robert Dreyfus that he had worked at *Contre Sainte-Beuve* for sixty hours without a rest. Before departing for Normandy in mid-August he wrote a letter to Alfred Vallette, editor at Mercure de France, describing the contents of *Contre Sainte-Beuve:* "I am finishing a book which, despite its provisional title, 'Against Sainte-Beuve: Recollection of a Morning,' is a genuine novel and an extremely indecent one in places. One of the main characters is a homosexual. . . . The name Sainte-Beuve is not there by chance. The book does end with a long conversation about Sainte-Beuve and about aesthetics . . . and when one has finished the book, one will see (I hope) that the entire novel is nothing but the implementation of the artistic principles expressed in this final part, a sort of introduction, if you like, inserted at the end. . . . It is a book that chronicles events, and the reflection that events have on one another over intervals of years."[21] Sight unseen,

Vallette turned it down. Proust then approached Calmette of the *Figaro*, who expressed only tentative interest in publishing an excerpt.

Before the journey to Cabourg in August he arranged for his bedroom to be lined with cork, but then canceled the plan for fear of not being away long enough. An all-important letter to Mme Straus from this moment makes the following declaration: "I've just begun—and finished—the whole of a long book"—by which he means "Combray" plus much of the second half of what will be *Time Regained*—in other words, the two ends of his great bridge. Proust's claim that he wrote the conclusion of the *Search* before the beginning turns out to be more nearly true than people have supposed.

The big book announced to Mme Straus—referred to as *Contre Sainte-Beuve* but not the miscellany published posthumously in the 1950s under that title—would fill twenty-one composition books and a hoard of loose sheets and consume virtually every waking hour between the end of 1908 and the end of 1909.[22] The novel was conceived as the narrative of a *grasse matinée*, a leisurely morning in bed. First the Narrator is seen tossing and turning and waiting for daybreak and his mother. He remembers a place called Combray where he passed holidays in his childhood, exploring its two different paths, and got to know a man named Swann. He also remembers Querqueville (later Balbec), a seaside retreat where he and his mother met her old school friend Mme de Villeparisis and her nephew Montargis (later Saint-Loup).

The Narrator's mother arrives at his bedside bearing a newspaper in which something he wrote has been published, presumably his first appearance in print. He hears the cries of hawkers in the street and contemplates a journey to Venice with his mother. The Comtesse de Guermantes, who lives at the opposite end of the courtyard and is the object of the Narrator's idealized love, coexists in his heart with more mundane fantasies about working-class and peasant girls he's been observing.

As well, the manuscript included a first version of the Verdurin circle; a homosexual marquis named de Guercy (Proust's first go at Charlus); and a little girl named Gilberte and her mother. The novel, in this original conception, was to have ended with son and mother discussing Balzac, Baudelaire, and Nerval and coming to large-scale conclusions about the nature of art, conclusions that would annihilate forever the biographical determinism of Charles Augustin Sainte-Beuve.

Readers of *In Search of Lost Time* will be struck by the familiarity of all these elements. Proust's mature masterpiece was taking shape with preternatural speed. As for the last item, the argument against Sainte-Beuve, it will not so much disappear as get dispersed into the *Search:* Mme de Villeparisis, Bloch, and M. de Norpois all parrot Sainte-Beuve's view that biography is the only way to understand an author. "It was while denouncing the critic," writes Carter, "that Proust made the key discovery in his long apprenticeship to become a creative person."[23] He had ceased to be an essayist or critic or anything but a novelist. As fictional imagination more and more drove out belles lettres, the title *Contre Sainte-Beuve* grew less and less relevant. At last, having no more use for the polemic he began with, Marcel returned the copy of Sainte-Beuve's *Port-Royale* he had borrowed from Lauris. Out of a polemical article of doubtful urgency on a literary critic who died two years before Marcel was born, the greatest novel ever written was coming to birth.

The *cahiers* from this season are purposeful, rigorous, self-assured; *Jean Santeuil* seems invertebrate by comparison. Nowhere in *Santeuil* were Proust's burgeoning gifts for satire and grotesque portraiture. And he had benefited hugely from the shift to first person. But the most important change was that he now had more than just episodes; he was now possessed by the story he had to tell. Such years as remained—notwithstanding torments of love, deaths of friends, the all-transforming tragedy of world war—were a solitary emergency consecrated to the darkness and silence of creative imagination. With neither youth nor health to count on, Proust's one and only task was to carry through to completion his hard-won vision of the whole.

Chapter Eight

On January 21, 1910, after days of continuous rainfall, the sewers and subways of Paris filled to bursting. A flood like none the city had ever known engulfed the streets, lasting for nearly two weeks. Shelters were improvised in the upper floors of schools and churches. Firefighters and laborers took to the streets in boats to rescue people from second-story windows. Within Gare d'Orsay stood a lake one meter deep. Only quick construction of levees by state engineers, working alongside ordinary citizens, kept the Seine from spilling over its quai walls and producing a much worse catastrophe. Makeshift boardwalks appeared, many the work, again, of ordinary Parisians responding to the emergency. At the Comédie-Française performances went on by the light of acetylene lamps. One sees to this day plaques marking the high-water mark (8.62 meters, or 28.28 feet) reached on January 28.

In March, probably at Mme Straus's *salon,* Proust met a

twenty-year-old young man little like himself at that age, Jean Cocteau—dazzlingly self-possessed, professional, and omnibrilliant—whom he would much later recall as having "the look of a siren with his delicate fish-bone nose and his fascinating eyes. Also the look of a seahorse."[1] Reviewing Lucien Daudet's *Le Prince des cravates* that autumn (favorably, of course—this was a former lover), he would also take note of Cocteau, author of *Le Prince frivole*, as one "whom a higher destiny awaits."[2]

In his memoir *Opium* here is how Cocteau recalls Proust: "I can see him, bearded, seated on a red bench at Larue's. . . . I can see him, without a beard, at the home of Mme Alphonse Daudet, being pestered by [Francis] Jammes, who buzzed around him like a horsefly. I can see him again, on his deathbed, with the beginnings of a beard. I see him, both with and without a beard, in that cork-lined bedroom with its dust and its phials, either in bed wearing gloves or standing in a bathroom that looked a likely setting for a crime, buttoning a velvet waistcoat over his poor square chest, which appeared to contain his clockwork spring. Still standing, he ate a dish of noodles. I see him surrounded by dust-sheets. They covered the chandelier and the armchairs. . . . I see him leaning against the mantelpiece in the drawing-room of this Nautilus."[3]

How enchanting, how like Cocteau, to equate Marcel at boulevard Haussmann to Jules Verne's Captain Nemo in his submarine. And, yes, the bedroom had finally been lined with cork—"a little bottle stop"[4] against the noise of the world—in July and August of 1910, while he was away at Cabourg, accompanied that year by his valet, Nicolas Cottin. Before departing, Marcel had attended the first night of the Ballets Russes, back for their second Paris season, with Nijinsky and Ida Rubinstein dancing in Fokine's *Shéhérazade* and Tamara Karsavina and Fokine together in the *Firebird*. A week later he returned as Mme Greffulhe's guest to see *La Sylphide* and *Cléopâtre*.

A less pleasant excursion, at one in the morning, had been

to the *Figaro* offices of Gaston Calmette—eventually the dedicatée of *Swann's Way* but no enthusiast for Proust's work at this stage—in order to retrieve a typescript of the book he was still calling *Contre Sainte-Beuve.* Calmette had no interest, as it turned out, in publishing any of its contents. And an additional challenge to self-confidence in these months would be the appearance of Binet-Valmer's explicitly homosexual novel *Lucien.* Proust worried that a more prolific and better-known author had scooped him.

Add to these a social wound: Georges de Lauris, for so many years a great friend and confidant, and Marcel's literary executor, refused to invite him to his wedding. Proust always regarded the marriage of any male friend as a personal catastrophe, true, but would have wanted to be there. Tadié has suggested, not implausibly, that the aristocratic Lauris could not abide Marcel's clothes and general appearance, but one cannot know. Further cause for sadness was a curt rupture with Antoine Bibesco, whose misdeed was to have suggested that Marcel might be more than just a disinterested observer of the love that dared not speak its name.[5] And perhaps the ultimate blow to *amour propre* came when he realized that Lucien Daudet, his old flame, had taken up with the glittering Cocteau.

Yet no setback could impair Proust's creative pace. Far from it. The heroic work of 1910, as reflected in the *cahiers,* can be summarized as follows: revisions and expansions to "Combray" and to "Querqueville" (the original of the Balbec portions of *In the Shadow of Young Girls in Flower*); revisions and expansions to "Swann in Love" and "Madame Swann at Home"; and—momentously—a first draft of *The Guermantes Way. Cahiers* 57 and 58 were shortly to contain what becomes the finale to *In Search of Lost Time,* the afternoon party at the Paris residence of the Princess de Guermantes. In other words, the whole of the architecture of the *Search* was already there.

Proust was meanwhile taking inspiration from Hardy's *A*

Pair of Blue Eyes, his bedside book that autumn, as well as carefully annotating Stendhal's *Charterhouse*, from Balzac's introduction to which the struggling, unknown novelist may well have drawn solace: "Above all other professions, artists have an invincible *self-love*, an artistic sentiment and indelible consciousness of things. . . . The writer and the painter remain always faithful to their genius, even face to face with the scaffold."[6] And finally the important matter of a noble name Proust wanted but hesitated to invoke had finally been settled when François de Pâris wrote to certify that the last Duc de Guermantes died in 1800. Proust communicated his thanks, adding that he intended "both to exalt and to sully" the defunct name.[7]

Early in 1911 he took out a subscription to the so-called Théâtrophone service enabling housebound people to listen by telephone to performances at the Opéra, the Opéra-Comique, the Concerts Colonne, and the Comédie-Française. By this means, on February 21, he heard Debussy's *Pelléas and Mélisande*, which mesmerized him. The best thing since Félix Mayol, he announced to Reynaldo, which may have set the latter's teeth on edge; Mayol was a sissified cabaret singer famed for such entertaining nonsense as "Viens, poupoule!"

Reynaldo had moved ahead as if on invisible wires, winning commissions from Diaghilev and acclaim in Saint Petersburg, sought after both as composer and as conductor. But Marcel was turning forty with little to show. On July 11, 1911, following a cheerless birthday, he departed for Cabourg, where he would spend the next three months. There he hired a Miss Cecilia Hayward to type the novel—now entitled *Les Intermittences du Coeur* and conceived as part one of a long work he intended to call *Le Temps Perdu*—using not the *cahiers* but a fair copy made by Albert Nahmias, a young man Proust had met back in the summer of the young men in flower and later hired as his secretary. Handsome and attentive, Albert naturally became the focus of Marcel's affections. In April 1912 he wrote: "I seem to see, beneath the center-part of your hair, the smile in your eyes on your good days, and that distention, that flaring of the nostrils that in you is a sign of benevolence and also, when it occurs, a great embellishment."[8] Albert, who lived a long life and died at Cannes in 1979, would be among the last living links to Proust. When asked whether he was the model for Albertine Simonet, the Narrator's supreme love, Nahmias would gracefully reply, "There were several of us."[9]

Revising the fair copy cheek by jowl with Miss Hayward as she typed—for her French was terrible and every word required his supervision—Proust arrived at the first three hundred pages of *Swann's Way* pretty much as we know them. At the same time, he was drafting new material. In the fourth week of August he reported to Lauris that the book was now eight hundred pages long. So that settles it: Proust did indeed write the beginning and end of his novel simultaneously, correcting the first three hundred pages of *Swann's Way* even as he produced an early version of the afternoon party that concludes *Time Regained.*

On October 1 he returned to Paris to cope with major losses on the Bourse. Proust belonged, as Tadié says, "to that category of small investor who buys on a rising market and sells on the downturn."[10] A great deal of his inherited wealth would vanish as the result of foolish investments, not to mention a too lavish generosity to those around him. (On himself Marcel spent almost nothing.)

His health was worsening. Through the good offices of Dr. Émile Calmette, Proust's name was permanently removed from the active military service rolls. It is certainly hard to imagine what, in the event of war, his useful function would have been. When Reynaldo's mother died in March of 1912, Marcel was too fragile to attend the funeral. When Reynaldo conducted *Don Giovanni* at the Opéra-Comique Marcel again was too sick to be present. (Whether he listened by Théâtrophone is unknown.) On March 21 a housebound Proust had the pleasure of seeing in *Le Figaro* the first of four excerpts from, roughly speaking, *Swann's Way*. By late spring he was speaking of a manuscript fourteen hundred pages in length and, in a letter to novelist and poet Jean-Louis Vaudroyer, foresaw two volumes of seven hundred pages each, or perhaps five volumes of three hundred pages each. In a weird letter to Reynaldo he proposed sixteen possible titles for the work as a whole, among them *The Stalactites of the Past*, *In Front of a Few Stalactites of the Past* (as if the first weren't bad enough), *Reflections in a Patina*, *What One Sees in a Patina*, and others no more plausible in their French originals than in English.

* * *

"Amaze me," Serge Diaghilev would instruct the dancers of his Ballets Russes. The most conspicuous of them, Vaslav Nijinsky, did that and more on the evening of May 29, 1912, at the notorious première of *The Afternoon of a Faun*. The music was by Debussy after Mallarmé's poem; the iconoclastic choreography was Nijinsky's own. His masturbatory shudder at the conclusion drove Paris to extremes of indignation and rapture. Marcel had been present that evening, as he would be a year later at the premiere of *The Rite of Spring*, after which he would dine in Restaurant Larue with Stravinsky, Diaghilev, Nijinsky, and Cocteau.[11] Heady company, but his name would in time be as thunderous as these others'; for the bedside table of this seemingly unproductive lightweight and sleeper-in groaned with the notebooks of a masterwork that was to challenge the novel as decisively as Stravinsky had challenged music or Nijinsky had challenged ballet.

On June 4, the day *Le Figaro* published a second extract, "A Ray of Sunlight on the Balcony," Marcel braved a little sunlight himself in order to see at Bernheim-Jeune twenty-nine views of Venice by the living painter he most admired, Monet. On June 27 Miss Hayward arrived bearing the 712-page typescript. Now thinking in terms of three volumes, Marcel reported to Geneviève Straus that he wished to call the first *Le Temps perdu* and the third *Le Temps retrouvé.* In a November letter to Gaston Gallimard he firmly proposed three volumes: "For example, overall title *Les Intermittances du Coeur.* First volume, subtitle: *Le Temps Perdu.* Second volume, subtitle: *L'Adoration perpétuelle* (or perhaps *À l'ombre des jeunes filles en fleurs*). Third volume, subtitle: *Le Temps retrouvé.*"[12] *Le Figaro* published the next extract, "The Village Church," on its front page for September 1. In late October, in a letter to Antoine, with whom he had reconciled, Proust wondered whether Gallimard's NRF would be the right house for his novel: "I'd pay for the edition as handsomely as they wish. From the literary point of view (although I suspect that, for reasons I believe to be false, they may not estimate me at my true worth, which isn't great but higher than they may think) I won't disgrace them."[13] Here was a fresh outbreak of the old naïveté, Marcel assuming that because it was offered *à compte d'auteur*—at the author's expense—NRF and Gallimard would have no objection. His friend Louis de Robert had to explain bluntly what was obvious to everyone else: Such munificence implied that the work was otherwise unpublishable.

Proust also sounded out Eugène Fasquelle, publisher of Flaubert, Zola, the Goncourts, and warned him of a homosexual character in the book who "puts on a show of virility, of contempt for effeminate young men, etc. But in the second part this elderly gentleman of a noble family reveals himself as a pederast who will be portrayed in a comic light, but without any obscene language. He will be seen 'picking up' a concierge and 'keeping' a pianist."[14] The deeper interest of such a character, so different from what he seems at first, is the theme of metamorphosis in a novel *necessarily* vast in length, as it means to show the effects of time on a very large cast of characters. Marcel would claim Dostoyevsky—above all the Dostoyevsky of

The Idiot—as his great teacher in this art of revealing people, by progressive effect, to be the opposite of what they originally seem.

On Christmas Eve both Fasquelle and NRF rejected the book. Fasquelle's reader, Jacques Normand, wrote in his report: "712-page manuscript . . . one has no notion—none—of what it is about. What is it all for? What does it all mean? Where is it all leading?—It's impossible to know! It's impossible to say!"[15]

The reader's report for NRF was by none other than Gide. He briefly sampled the manuscript before rejecting it. (Gide's later claim to Céleste Albaret that the package was never opened at NRF is false.)

Reeling from the shock of two rejections, Proust sounded much like others who've tried and failed to find a publisher—as full of chagrined explanations as he'd earlier been of exalted hopes. In early January Paul Ollendorff, chiefly a publisher of nature books, added his rejection to the pile. So insulting was this one that Robert de Flers, who'd approached Ollendorff on Proust's behalf, hesitated to show it, requesting from Robert Humblot, Ollendorff's editor in chief, something milder than the reader's report of one George Boyer, theater critic at *Le Petit Journal:* "I may be dead from the neck up, but cudgel my brains as I may, I fail to understand why a man needs thirty pages to describe how he tosses and turns in bed before falling asleep."[16]

Proust also attempted to place extracts in the May number of *La Nouvelle Revue Française*, the periodical of Gallimard's publishing firm. Jacques Copeau, the editor, turned him down. This, in retrospect, may be seen as the nadir. Proust's luck changed when he requested from René Blum, younger brother of Léon Blum and editor of the magazine *Gil Blas*, an introduction to Bernard Grasset. Here is his appeal of February 23: "This book is a novel; at least, it's from the novel form that it departs least."[17] Blum arranged the submission and within four days Grasset, publisher of such younger talent as Giraudoux, Mauriac, and Cocteau, agreed without reading to publish *Swann's Way*, albeit at the author's expense.

Someone had finally taken Marcel up on his embarrassing offer. As simply as that, the drama was over.

* * *

In the spring of 1913 he hired Alfred Agostinelli, the "mechanic" he'd first known in Normandy six years earlier, as his typist, a position for which Alfred was not notably qualified. It seems there was some anxiety about hurting the feelings of another member of the household staff, Odilon Albaret, who drove Proust on those occasions when he did go out and would not have responded well to someone else with the title of chauffeur, as the word now was. Thus as "typist" Alfred moved to boulevard Haussmann with Anna, supposedly his wife. (She was not. Anna Square was her name and everybody hated her. Indeed, Odilon called her "the flying louse.") In a letter to Charles d'Alton Proust wrote that he had shaved his beard "so as to alter my features a little for the person I have met again."[18] Now sleek and darkly handsome, Alfred had captured Proust's heart. Looking back in June of 1914, he would write to Émile Straus: "It was then that I discovered him, and that he and his wife became an integral part of my existence."[19] (Exquisitely courteous of Marcel to include the flying louse here. One may guess what his feelings about her were.)

The first of five sets of page proofs arrived from Grasset in early April. Correcting them, Proust developed a new method of revision described in a letter to Vaudoyer: "I stick additional bits of paper above and below, to the right and the left, etc."[20]—a first mention of what Céleste will call Monsieur Proust's "paperolles." In the last week of May he wrote decisively to Grasset that "the first part will be called *Du côté de chez Swann.* The second part probably *Le Côté de Guermantes.* The overall title of the two volumes: *À la recherche du temps perdu.*" He'd abandoned *Les Intermittances du Coeur* as the overall title after seeing an announcement for Binet-Valmer's *Le Coeur en désordre,* soon to appear. As to the change of title for volume one, some regretted the abandonment of *Le Temps Perdu* in favor of *Du côté de chez Swann,* which seemed pedestrian by comparison—literally so, as it means "the walk by Swann's house." Proust responded, not very accurately, that *Le Rouge et le noir, Connaissance de l'est, Les Nourritures terrestres* and *L'Annonce faite à Marie* were also nonpoetic titles. Nearly as significant was where the break between volumes one and two should come: "I cannot cut the book as easily as a lump of butter," he wrote to Grasset in late June.[21] But cut like so much butter the product would have to be: *Swann's Way* as he proposed it was too big to publish; "Madame Swann at Home," which he'd intended as the final movement of volume one, would instead be the opening of *In the Shadow of Young Girls in Flower.*

Venturing out that April to the Salle Villiers, Proust heard César Franck's 1886 Sonata in A Major for Piano and Violin, the rondo of which, with its lilting call and response, was to be one model for the composer Vinteuil's little phrase ("piano and violin moan like birds calling to each other")[22] in the *Search.* Such pleasures were not to be had via Théâtrophone. Both that device and a recently purchased pianola had palled on him. Of the latter he wrote to Mme Straus: "They happen not to have the pieces I want to play. Beethoven's sublime fourteenth quartet does not appear among the rolls."[23] And he would say goodbye to the Théâtrophone the following year when he ordered all telephone services removed from the boulevard Haussmann apartment.

Chapter Nine

"One must wait a long time before the public becomes accustomed to our language,"[1] Stravinsky said about his music and Nijinsky's choreography after the explosive première of *The Rite of Spring* on May 29, 1913, at the newly completed Théatre des Champs-Elysées, a stunning modern hall in the style soon to be called Deco. Jeers and hisses grew so loud it was hard for the dancers to hear the orchestra; Nijinsky resorted to shouting out the step numbers; Pierre Monteux soldiered on in the pit. "A laborious and puerile barbarity," announced *Le Figaro* the following day. Proust had watched it all from the audience.

A momentous year for ballet, 1913. For aviation too. On September 23, a mere decade after Orville and Wilbur Wright briefly got aloft at Kitty Hawk, news of Roland Garros crossing the Mediterranean flashed round the world. Young Alfred Agostinelli, green as grass, saw himself doing comparable feats.

His automotive background would make aviation a cinch, he felt. Helplessly in love with the young man—in love, evidently, as never before—Proust was presently paying for Agostinelli's lessons at Garros's flying school southwest of Paris. Having already promised Alfred a Rolls-Royce, he seems now to have upped the ante to an airplane. All this for a cunning and ignorant boy with no love to offer in return. But as Proust says in "Swann in Love," probity in matters of the heart is "invariably shown by clever people who, not being in love themselves, feel that a clever man should only be unhappy about a person who is worth his while; which is rather like being astonished that anyone should condescend to die of cholera at the bidding of so insignificant a creature as the common bacillus."[2]

A vital new member of the household made her first appearance that September. On a visit to the village of Auxillac, his birthplace in Lozère, Odilon Albaret had wooed and won a girl named Céleste Gineste—who knew nothing of the larger world, had never even seen a city—and brought her to Paris as his bride. She would be the most loving and best person Marcel Proust was to know in his remaining nine years of life.

* * *

After a short season in Cabourg he returned to boulevard Haussmann. The following month Grasset officially announced *Swann's Way* as volume one of a three-volume novel, with subsequent installments to be called *The Guermantes Way* and *Time Regained.* In an early November letter to René Blum, Proust declared that his book was "very different from what you know of me, I think, and infinitely less feeble, no longer deserving the epithet 'delicate' or 'sensitive' but living and true."[3] Proust would urge Calmette at the *Figaro* not to identify his book as being by the author of *Pleasures and Days*, nor to employ the words "fine" or "delicate" when describing it. He greatly feared that the old caricature—effeminate sentimental dabbler, vainly preoccupied with a cosseted childhood—might endure. To Jacques Copeau at the *Nouvelle Revue Française* he wrote: "The attitude of a dilettante who is content to delight in the memory of things is the *opposite* of mine."[4]

A week before publication Proust sat for an interview with Élie-Joseph Bois of *Le Temps:* "It is the invisible substance of time that I have tried to isolate, and it meant that the experiment had to last over a long period. . . . My work is based on the distinction between involuntary and voluntary memory."[5] This, he said, set his philosophy apart from Bergson's, or anyone's. He wished to emphasize that *In Search of Lost Time* would be not merely a new kind of novel but a new comprehension of life.

A week later in *Le Miroir* André Lévy (who wrote as André Arnyvelde) made the first public mention of a cork-lined room. But Proust, beset by unhappy love for the constantly present and always out-of-reach Alfred, was hankering now for other rooms, apparently grander ones, and pipe-dreamed for himself a splendid escape. To Jean-Louis Vaudoyer he declared that he would like to find "a quiet, isolated house in Italy" to retreat to. "You don't happen to know if that Farnese palace (the Cardinal's), at a place which I think is called Caprarola, is to let?"[6]

November 14, publication day, was also the first official day of Céleste Albaret's employment at 102, boulevard Haussmann. Her assignment was to deliver copies of *Swann's Way* to various of Marcel's friends. Bernard Grasset, meanwhile, was unkindly warning people that the book had been funded by its author and was unreadable. Reynaldo, on the other hand, accurately stated Marcel's achievement in a letter: "It is *without a doubt* (and here my friendship plays no part) *the finest book* to appear since *L'Éducation sentimentale.* From *the first line* a *great genius* reveals itself and since this opinion one day will be universal, we must get used to it at once."[7]

The readers Proust cared most about were strongly favorable. In *Excelsior* Cocteau wrote that the book "resembles nothing I know and reminds me of everything I admire"—an excellent description of any great original work that emerges from and transcends an accumulated tradition. From Francis Jammes came an admiring letter that Proust particularly cherished. The only sour note was in *Le Temps*, which ran a vicious attack by Paul Souday. (Years later, this same critic would claim to have discovered Marcel Proust.)[8] Another minor light, Henri Ghéon, sought to trivialize *Swann's Way* in the *Nouvelle Review Française*. But Proust would soon be a writer the men at NRF cherished—indeed above all others, as letters in the early weeks of 1914 from Gide ("The rejection of this book will remain the gravest mistake ever made by the NRF")[9] and Jacques Rivière ("I shall never forget the wonderment, the depth of emotion into which I was plunged")[10] attested. The *Nouvelle Review Française* would shortly publish an excerpt from the first stay at Balbec and, in the following issue, further set pieces, including the death of the grandmother.

Grasset's first edition contained at least a thousand misprints. Impresario and journalist Gabriel Astruc, one of Proust's earliest and most passionate devotées, volunteered his meticulously annotated copy for use in preparing a corrected second run. Proust had meanwhile kept writing, getting a typed version of what he at this time considered volume two, and also completing in exercise books the second stay at Balbec.

And now Alfred Agostinelli and Anna Square fled to Monte Carlo—as if for their lives. Marcel would never see his beloved again. And now the name Albertine, which will recur 2,360 times in the course of the *Search*, appeared in the *cahiers*. "The person we love is to be recognized only by the intensity of pain that we suffer," he was to write in *In the Shadow of Young Girls in Flower*.[11] The pain suffered after Alfred's departure was deranging. Marcel engaged a private detective to find the couple, and dispatched Nahmias (as the Narrator will dispatch Saint-Loup in *The Fugitive*, volume six of the cycle) to try to bribe

Alfred's father (as Saint-Loup will try to bribe Albertine's aunt) into forcing the young man to return to boulevard Haussmann. The imaginative elements for the Albertine love saga were leaping to life even as Marcel's love for Agostinelli hurried to its tragic conclusion.

* * *

"At last," he wrote to Rivière, the most talented young critic in France, "I find a reader who has *grasped* that my book is a dogmatic work with a structure. . . . I thought it more honorable and tactful as an artist not to let it be seen, not to proclaim that I was setting out precisely in search of the Truth, nor to say what it consisted in for me. I so hate those ideological works in which the narrative is a constant betrayal of the author's intentions that I preferred to say nothing. It's only at the end of the book, when the lessons of life have been grasped, that my design will become clear."[12] Similarly, he told Gide that he wrote exclusively about those things in which he perceived "a general truth."[13]

The novel in progress was as far as one could get from Art for Art's Sake. Art for Truth's Sake was now the goal.

In mid-March came an important letter from Gide, who'd returned from Florence to attend an editorial meeting at which the NRF board unanimously voted to take on the whole of the *Search*, including a new edition of *Swann's Way*, as soon as Grasset's current print run was exhausted. The latter had released Proust from his (murky) contractual obligation and confirmed authorial ownership of the whole—at which point Proust was so moved that he decided to remain with Grasset, meanwhile continuing to dicker with NRF. It is not for business acumen that we celebrate Marcel Proust.

* * *

On March 16, at six in the evening, Gaston Calmette, the dedicatée of *Swann's Way*, was murdered in the offices of the

Figaro by Henriette Caillaux, wife of Joseph Caillaux, minister of finance, against whom the paper had conducted a smear campaign, reporting that his sexual relations with the current Mme Caillaux began when he was still married to her predecessor. In the best tradition of French jurisprudence, Henriette Caillaux would be acquitted on grounds that her crime was one of passion.

Far more preoccupying for Marcel than Calmette's bizarre death was the ongoing agony of Agostinelli's disappearance. Sometime in early spring the young man had enrolled in an aviation school run by the Garbero brothers at La Grimaudière, near Antibes. Strange to say, Alfred registered there under the name "Marcel Swann"—a gesture that will bear as much interpretation as one cares to heap upon it but is finally mysterious. Proust would now play the trump card in his effort to reclaim the young man. On May 28 he asked Hauser to liquidate twenty thousand francs' worth of his Suez holdings in order to buy an airplane. On the same day, he called on Ferdinand Collin, director of the flying school Alfred had attended, to discuss the purchase. Meanwhile back at La Grimaudière two days later, at about five in the afternoon, Alfred took off on his second solo flight over the Bay of Angels. Banking very low, he caught a wing on the water. His plane was pulled down. Alfred, who could not swim, climbed out onto the wreckage and called for help. Horrified onlookers, Anna among them, watched as the monoplane suddenly went under. Alfred's body was found eight days later; he carried on his person six thousand francs, what remained of his employer's fatal munificence.

Proust mastered his terrible grief—which he likened to what he'd endured after Jeanne's death—sufficiently to call on Collin, Alfred's instructor. Refusing Collin's offer of reimbursement for the lessons paid for but not taken, he declared himself, as Collin reports it, entirely "responsible for the death of the young pilot." Collin continues: "He begged me to accept this sum in memory of the fatal weakness he had shown in yielding to the entreaties of his secretary, who dreamed of nothing but aviation."[14]

A single letter from Proust to Alfred survives, the rest having been destroyed by the Agostinellis.[15] In it he delicately threatens to cancel the airplane that has just been ordered and also to cancel some other princely item, probably a Rolls-Royce—as in *The Fugitive* the Narrator attempts to lure Albertine back with a yacht and a Rolls.

Between June 6 and 11 Grasset set proof pages of *The Guermantes Way*, a title that will never appear with the contents planned at this time; they are instead pretty much those of *In the Shadow of Young Girls in Flower* as we know it and not to be confused with the volumes called *The Guermantes Way* that ultimately appear. But the house of Grasset, like other publishers, suddenly suspended operations owing to the international crisis triggered by the assassination at Sarajevo of Archduke Franz Ferdinand and his wife on June 28: "the thunderbolt of the Austro-Serbian incident," as Proust called it.[16] Europe's Belle Époque perished in the ensuing weeks. What ought to have been a conflict between Austria-Hungary and the Kingdom of Serbia, simply another Balkan war, became World War I, a calamity engineered by men who imagined themselves masters of the unfolding events, only to be mastered by them. That they were blind and unwitting perpetrators, history's playthings, is now clear to all students of the second decade of the twentieth century. The gunshots at Sarajevo, Russia's pledge to "little Serbia"; Kaiser Wilhelm's goading of Austria-Hungary into retributive demands; Great Britain's determination not to let the North Sea and North Atlantic become German waters; the kaiser's dream of conquering France as neatly as had his grandfather forty-one years earlier in the Franco-Prussian War: Such were the July ingredients that produced 1,566 days of unprecedented warfare and seventeen million military and civilian deaths.

There was nothing in post-Napoleonic Europe's frame of reference for a conflict lasting so long or producing such hecatombs. But on August 2, the day France mobilized all able-bodied men up to age forty-five in response to Germany's violation of Belgian neutrality, Proust wrote a letter to Lionel Hauser in which he envisaged a conflagration in which "millions of men are going to be massacred in a war of the worlds comparable to that of Wells."[17] At midnight on the evening of mobilization, he waved his brother out of Gare de l'Est. By now a distinguished surgeon in civilian life, Robert had requested front-line duty at the Verdun hospital. In the terrible haste that evening he asked Marcel to look after his wife and child and to inform his mistress, a Mme Fournier, of his departure. Next day the Second Reich declared war on France, and one day later Great Britain, citing the violation of Belgian neutrality, declared war on Germany.

From Robert there was no word for more than two months. Proust would have to wait until October to learn that his brother, now with the rank of captain in the Medical Corps, had been a surgeon at Étain—a town to the northeast of Verdun destroyed by the Germans—where under fire in August he had heroically kept the field hospital in operation. Reading seven newspapers a day for war news, Proust recoiled from the jingoistic hatred of Germany flourishing on the opinion pages: "'Boche' doesn't figure in my vocabulary," he declared.[18] He wrote to Hauser in August of 1915 that the press is "greatly inferior to the great things it speaks about." (An exception to the general censure was Henri Bidou's column, "The Military Situation," in *Le Journal des Débats.* For Bidou, Proust formed a keen admiration and some of his style and point of view find their way into Saint-Loup's military observations in *The Guermantes Way.*)

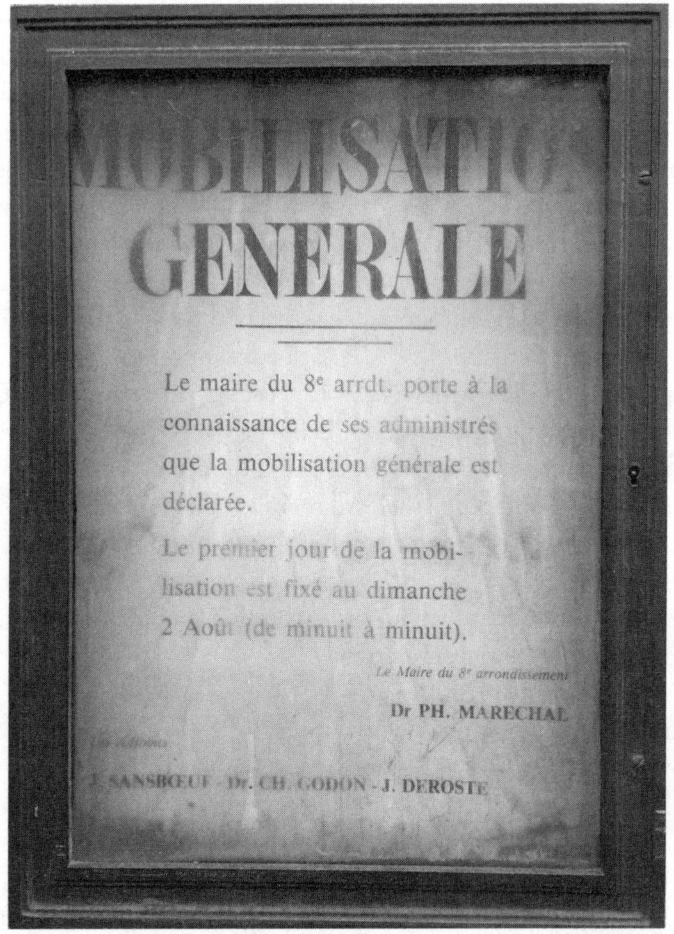

Notice of General Mobilization, August 2, 1914. Benjamin Taylor

A late-night walk through Paris brought home how starkly vulnerable to destruction the city was. The language of his letters from these early months of war is nearly identical to a passage in *Time Regained* in which the Narrator takes a similar walk: "The moonlight was like a soft and steady magnesium flare, by the light of which some camera might, for the last time, have been recording nocturnal images of those lovely groups of buildings like the Place Vendôme and the Place de la Concorde, to which my fear of the shells that were perhaps about to destroy them imparted by contrast, as they stood in their still intact beauty, a sort of plenitude, as if they were bending forward and freely offering their defenseless architecture to the blows that might fall."[19]

On September 3 Proust journeyed to Cabourg—it would be his last stay there—with Céleste and Ernest Forssgren, his new Swedish manservant. The train was packed and there were even people riding on the roofs of the cars. Parisians were convinced that their city was about to fall. As it turned out, German forces would be driven back to the Marne, setting the stage for France's first great battle of the war. Twenty-two hours after setting out, Proust, Céleste, and Forssgren arrived at the Grand-Hôtel to find the casino shuttered and the dining room and first two floors transformed into an auxiliary hospital. Proust wrote to Lucien that he'd given such cash as he had to the wounded.[20]

Next day the First Battle of the Marne began. Among the dead would be Jacques Rivière's brother-in-law, Henri-Alban Fournier, famed as Alain-Fournier for his novel *Le Grand Meaulnes* (a far greater commercial success in 1913 than *Swann's Way* had been), who fell at Saint-Rémy-la-Calonne. Dead as well, at Villeroy-sur-Marne, was Charles Péguy. In six days of fighting along three hundred miles of riverfront, the Miracle on the Marne (as Frenchmen called it after their victory) claimed a quarter of a million German lives and as many French. No subsequent engagement of the war would average as many deaths per day.

It was a crushing strategic blow to General Helmuth von Moltke's aim of seizing Paris and demanding terms. Had that happened Germany could have concentrated on the struggle with Russia, and won, and the course of the twentieth century would be unrecognizably different. But the Marne deprived Wilhelm II of the quick victory over France he'd anticipated.

* * *

In mid-October, Proust returned from Cabourg to Paris, which he would never leave again. The most wrenching news of all reached him there in December when his friend Bertrand de Fénelon—"His Blue Eyes" of old—went missing at Mametz while commanding the 236th Infantry Regiment. Three months later came confirmation that Bertrand had been shot through the head while leading his men. Here is Proust in a letter to Antoine Bibesco: "I think about him so much that, having fallen asleep for an instant, I saw him and told him that I had thought he was dead. He was very delightful. Oh, that he and I could have such a conversation in reality!"[21] Almost immediately, Proust began to write of the heroic death of Robert de Saint-Loup, who, covering the retreat of his men in *Time Regained*, advances to attack a trench "out of generosity and because it was his habit to place at the service of others all that he possessed."[22]

Bertrand's death would be the hardest of the war for Proust, though by no means the only. Robert d'Humières fell at Lizerne, near Ypres. Translator of Kipling and Conrad and in the midst of translating Edith Wharton's *The Custom of the Country* at his death, he'd warmly assisted Proust with both Ruskin translations. "Under threat of a homosexual scandal," Carter writes, "d'Humières had asked to be posted to a Zouave regiment at the front."[23] And there was Gaston Arman de Caillavet's unexpected death from natural causes early in 1915.

Not surprisingly, these losses put into perspective the grief Proust continued to feel for Agostinelli. In the aftermath of the Marne he wrote to Reynaldo that having passed through "a first stage of disengagement" he could now think of the young man without pain.[24] Meanwhile the Albertine story was growing to vast proportions: *Cahier* 71 contains a first version of what will be *The Captive*, and *cahiers* 54 and 71 show *The Fugitive* taking shape. Also in 54 are drafts of the Charlus material. In *carnets* 3 and 4 Proust was sketching ideas about a quartet by Vinteuil, later the septet of *The Captive*. And he had been reading Joseph Reinach's *Histoire de l'affaire Dreyfus*, which would serve as his *aide-mémoire* for those years, now so distant. (Despite these researches certain aspects of the thorny Dreyfus chronology are going to trip him up in *The Guermantes Way*.)

Among the earliest admirers from abroad was Rainer Maria Rilke, who wrote to his editor, Anton Kippenberg, to report on *Du côté de chez Swann*, a "very important" and "incomparably remarkable" book composed in "an utterly original style," and advised Kippenberg to acquire it at the first opportunity for translation into German. In Italy Lucio d'Ambra wrote: "Remember this name and this title: Marcel Proust and *Du côté de chez Swann*. In fifty years, our children will place the name alongside Stendhal and the book alongside *Le Rouge et le noir* and the *Chartreuse*."[25] One of Proust's earliest American admirers, Edith Wharton, now living in Paris, had sent Henry James a copy of *Swann's Way*. In *A Backward Glance*, her autobiography, she would recall that James had "seized upon *Du côté de chez Swann* and devoured it in a passion of curiosity and admiration. Here, in the first volume of a long chronicle—the very type of the unrolling tapestry which was so contrary to his own conception of form—he instantly recognized a new vision, and a structural design as yet unintelligible to him, but as surely there as hard bone under soft flesh in a living organism. I wonder if in any other art the joy of such recognition is as great as it is to the born novelist who loves his craft, and sees its subtle and protean form so often stretched out of shape by insensitive hands. I look back with particular pleasure at having made Proust known to James, for the encounter gave him his last, and one of his strongest, artistic emotions."[26]

Chapter Ten

The name of Gaston Gallimard would not be enrolled among the brave of those years. Having tried and failed to get himself identified as "deceased" on the municipal register, he fasted to lose sixty pounds and feigned convulsions. On the evening of the day he was finally declared unfit for military service Gallimard went off to feast at Maxim's, evidently to excess, as he afterward vomited the meal onto rue Royale. He would comfortably sit out the war in Switzerland.[1]

On March 21, 1915, a new chapter of the conflict began with the first aerial raid on Paris. In *Time Regained* Saint-Loup, back from the front, asks the Narrator whether he had a good view of the Zeppelins on the previous night, "very much as in the old days he might have questioned me about some spectacle of great aesthetic beauty"—these early air raids being mere theater to Saint-Loup, who has seen the worst. "At the front, I could see, there might be a sort of bravado in saying: 'Isn't it marvelous! What a pink! And that pale green!' when at any moment you might be killed, but here in Paris there could be no such question of any such pose in Saint-Loup's way of speaking about an insignificant raid, which had in fact looked marvelously beautiful from our balcony when the silence of the night was broken by a display which was more than a display because it was real, with fireworks that were purposeful and protective and bugle-calls that did more than summon on parade."[2]

Proust says that a war is something that is lived like a love or a hatred and can be narrated like a novel. This global war, unlike any before it, was waged not just in Europe but in north China and the Falkland Islands, in German Southwest Africa, German East Africa, and British South Africa, throughout the Ottoman Near East, in India, in Indo-China. At the outset of hostilities General Charles Mangin had estimated that France could raise from its African and Asian possessions 300,000 troops for the western front, a number that was initially mocked. As it turned out, well above half a million French colonials were recruited to Europe. In the *Search*, upon the Narrator's second return to Paris following his lengthy stay at a sanatorium, he will behold—as Proust daily beheld—soldiers of every hue sporting trousers and headdresses from the ends of the earth, "an oriental scene which was at once meticulously accurate with respect to the costumes and the colours of the faces and arbitrarily fanciful when it came to the background, just as out of the town in which he lived Carpaccio made a Jerusalem or a Constantinople by assembling in its streets a crowd whose marvelous motley was not more rich in color than that of the crowd around me."[3] He spots Charlus trailing hungrily after a couple of Zouaves in their open-fronted jackets and red divided skirts.

Beginning in mid-April, British attempts to break the

trench stalemate at Neuve Chapelle, French attempts in Champagne and Artois and German attempts at Ypres all failed, resulting in massive casualties that did nothing to change the course of the conflict. On May 7, off the Irish coast, a German submarine torpedoed the British passenger ship *Lusitania*, sinking it within eighteen minutes; 1,198 civilian lives were lost. Proust's imagination put the event to use. In *Time Regained* the sinking of the *Lusitania* reveals as nowhere else the murky soul of Mme Verdurin. We learn that she has circumvented the laws rationing butter in order to obtain *prescription* croissants for her breakfast. Prone to sick headaches of aesthetical origin, she requires croissants as the remedy. One May morning, rattling her newspaper as she munches, Mme Verdurin reads of the disaster at sea. "'How horrible!' she said. 'This is something more horrible than the most terrible stage tragedy.' But the death of all these drowned people must have been reduced a thousand million times before it impinged upon her, for even as, with her mouth full, she made these distressful observations, the expression which spread over her face, brought there (one must suppose) by the savour of that so precious remedy against headaches, the croissant, was in fact one of satisfaction and pleasure."[4]

Here Mme Verdurin, rather than just being a comic villainess preoccupied more by a trivial indulgence than by the fate of twelve hundred souls, reminds us of how *bearable* the sufferings of others are—not just for a scoundrel like Mme Verdurin but for the rest of us too. Everyone knows from daily experience this unflattering truth. Mme Verdurin munching the croissant is no figure of fun. With the following, Proust makes her painfully one of us: "There is a law of inverse proportion which multiplies to such an extent anything that concerns our own welfare and divides by such a formidable figure anything that does not concern it, that the death of unknown millions is felt by us as the most insignificant of sensations, hardly even as disagreeable as a draught."[5]

* * *

"Night and day we think about the war," Proust wrote to his friend Charles d'Alton in May, "perhaps still more painfully when, like me, one is not taking part."[6] The state of Proust's health exempted him, though the threat of having his status reassessed was ever present. Meanwhile he read his seven newspapers.

Among those who had seen the horrors of the front was his publisher Grasset, now back in Paris and on his way to a Swiss hospital to convalesce from typhoid. Shocked by his appearance, Proust postponed speaking about the unsettled matter of the move to NRF. But it would be the final courtesy. Now that Proust was in demand, Grasset had served his purpose. "As in a fairy tale," Tadié writes, "everything was turned topsy-turvy: the very people who had not wanted *Du côté de chez Swann* now clamored for its sequel."[7] In November a more welcome visitor from the front was Reynaldo, who in the mire of the Vauquois trenches had composed his *Ruban dénoué*, a suite of waltzes for two pianos, and dedicated it "to the armies of 1915."

* * *

Proust was now hard at work on *Sodom and Gomorrah*, volume four of the cycle and the bombshell about which he'd warned prospective publishers. It was at this time that he incorporated the journey to Venice into *The Fugitive*, in which Venice stands not for loneliness and desolation but for the first stage of forgetting and the bliss of solitude. The Narrator's love for Albertine—for which Venice will be the cure—had turned real and anguishing from the moment it became jealous love, from the moment the Narrator's suspicion of Albertine's infidelities dawned. As for Swann, so for the Narrator: Love becomes an illness from which the lover must recover or die.

In "Madame Swann at Home," the first half of *In the Shadow of Young Girls in Flower*, Proust sets forth this credo in a single sentence: "The person whom we love is to be recognized only by the intensity of the pain we suffer."[8] Written well before the Albertine saga dawned on him, this compact wisdom prefigures the whole of it. Love's essence is the peril it exposes the lover to. In an important letter to Mme Scheikévitch, a Russian friend from Cabourg days, Proust lays out the entire Albertine story in November 1915: the suspicion, the exposure of lies, the conviction that he'd be better off were she dead, the dream of being alone, the desolation when his captive actually does flee.[9] The Narrator had various and trivial escapades in earlier drafts. But in the *Search* as we have it, his love for Albertine supplants these dalliances with high and dangerous Racinian passion. The dramatic gain is tremendous. As Proust says to Mme Scheikévitch, it is Albertine "who plays the biggest role and brings about the peripeteia."[10] (This Mme Scheikévitch, a woman whose nature greatly appealed to Proust, was no stranger to Racinian gestures. A few years earlier, in marital despair, she had shot herself through the chest with a revolver.)

* * *

"Alas," Proust wrote to Antoine Bibesco on New Year's Day, "1916 will have its violets and its apple blossoms, and before that its flowers flecked with frost, but there will never be a Bertrand again."[11] Nineteen-sixteen would be "the year of Verdun," in which eleven months of trench warfare—from January 21 to December 18—produced minor tactical gains. Three-quarters of a million French and German soldiers perished in the exercise. Proust spoke in a mid-February letter to Charles d'Alton of "this colossal geological convulsion"[12] rending them from the prewar past, a theme he'll take up in *Time Regained:* "One of the ideas most in vogue was that the pre-war days were separated from the war by something as profound, something that appeared to be as long-lasting as a geological period." The

Narrator then goes on to the following strange assertion: "The truth is that this profound change wrought by the war was in inverse proportion to the quality of the minds which it affected. . . . Those who have constructed an all-encompassing inner life for themselves have small regard for the importance of events."[13] But it is a claim belied by the book in which it appears. *Time Regained* incomparably reveals the Paris of the war years.

That February the Albertine story was glamorized with a new element: a collection of Fortuny gowns the Narrator drapes his beloved in. "I kissed her then a second time, pressing to my heart the shimmering golden azure of the Grand Canal and the mating birds, symbols of death and resurrection. But for the second time, instead of returning my kiss, she drew away with the sort of instinctive and baleful obstinacy of animals that feel the hand of death."[14] Proust had long admired the great Venetian designer and in *In the Shadow of Young Girls in Flower* has Elstir praise Fortuny's sumptuous brocades as rivaling those in Titian and Carpaccio. The Narrator must learn what Swann before him learned: that the beloved, whether in street clothes, in Fortuny gowns, or nude, is unknowable and unseizable, that in love one possesses nothing. Watching her in sleep he sees how fugitive Albertine is. Lovers learn, to their cost, that those they've chosen "are not immobile but in motion, and add to their person a sign corresponding to that which in physics denotes speed."[15] The merest look in the beloved's eyes intimates that she is elsewhere. "It is not even essential that we should have proof of her movement and flight, it is enough that we should guess them. She had promised us a letter. The letter has not come; each mail fails to bring it; what can have happened? Anxiety is born afresh, and love. It is such people more than any others who inspire love in us, to our desolation."[16]

But out of the martyrdom of wanting comes resurrection through separateness. Those Fortuny stuffs, with which the Narrator wishes to further ensnare the beloved, speak to him also of escape. Our hero will survive his dangerous love of Albertine and be reborn into a self-sufficient bliss that goes by the name of "Venice."

* * *

On February 25, 1916, the hatchet was officially buried between Proust and Gide, the latter having repented sufficiently of his initial rejection of the novel and reconfirmed NRF's offer to publish the whole. After a courtesy call one evening to boulevard Haussmann, he observed in his diary that it was the first time the two had set eyes on each other in twenty-four years.

That spring Proust asked the Poulet Quartet to come to boulevard Haussmann and play. Having secured their agreement, he and his driver collected all four musicians impromptu late one night and brought them to perform the Franck Quartet in D in his candlelit bedroom. When they finished the forty-five-minute piece Proust asked them to play it again. It was two in the morning, the quartet was exhausted, and Proust revived their spirits only with a very large gratuity. In April he attended the Festival Gabriel Fauré at the Odéon where Fauré's Quartet in C minor, op. 15, a favorite piece, was played. These two quartets—the Franck and the Fauré, music by his two favorite living composers—had already been of tremendous importance for the *Search*, though neither is the source of the little phrase of Vinteuil's sonata, so important for Swann, or of the reprise of it in Vinteuil's posthumous septet, so important for the Narrator.

In April of 1918 Proust would inscribe Jacques de Lacretelle's *de luxe* first edition of *Swann's Way*—one of five copies Grasset had printed on Japan Imperial paper—with a series of *clés* (keys) to the *Search*'s characters and invented musical compositions and works of architecture, assuring Lacretelle that there are "no keys to the characters of this book; or rather there are eight or ten for each one; the same is true of the church of Combray; many churches posed for me in memory. I no longer even remember whether the paving comes from

Saint-Pierre-sur-Dives or from Lisieux. Certain windows are certainly those of Évreux, others from the Sainte-Chapelle, and some from Pont-Audemer." And there followed this about the little phrase, for which he briefly claimed a single basis only to proustify or complicate the matter: "To whatever extent I made use of reality, actually, a very slight extent, . . . the little phrase of the sonata is, and I have never told this to anyone, the charming but infinitely mediocre phrase of a sonata for piano and violin by Saint-Saëns, a musician I don't like."[17] He then listed the Good Friday Spell from *Parsifal*, the prelude to *Lohengrin*, the Franck sonata for violin and piano, and an unspecified touch of Schubert—all music he revered—as contributing to the fictional music of Vinteuil.

As a young man Proust had internalized Schopenhauer's argument that music "reproduces all the emotions of our innermost being but entirely without reality and remote from its pain."[18] It is in the course of the Verdurins' musical evening in "Swann in Love" that the little phrase first enters the action.[19] Swann is galvanized by five notes recurring in the andante of Vinteuil's sonata in F-major, the offering of the evening, and names it the national anthem of his love for Odette. Swann "began to realize how much that was painful, perhaps even how much secret and unappeased sorrow underlay the sweetness of the phrase; and yet to him it brought no suffering."[20] Later, in the great scene at the Marquise de Sainte-Euverte's, he hears the piece yet again and attempts to kiss the little phrase as it wafts by: "As though the musicians were not nearly so much playing the little phrase as performing the rites on which it insisted before it would consent to appear, and proceeding to utter the incantations necessary to procure, and to prolong for a few moments, the miracle of its apparition, Swann, who was no more able to see it than if it had belonged to the world of ultra-violet light, and who experienced something like the refreshing sense of a metamorphosis in the momentary blindness with which he was struck as he approached it, Swann felt its presence like that of a protective goddess, a confidante of his love, who, in order to be able to come to him through the crowd and to draw him aside to speak to him, had disguised herself in this sweeping cloak of sound."[21]

A generation later it is the Narrator who harkens ecstatically—Swann-like—in *The Captive* to the little phrase when it unexpectedly reappears in a performance, again at the Verdurins', of Vinteuil's music, this time the septet, unpublished in his lifetime: "Where had he learned this song, different from those of other singers, similar to all his own, where had he heard it? Each artist seems thus to be the native of an unknown country, which he himself has forgotten, and which is different from that whence another great artist, setting sail for the earth, will eventually emerge. Certain it was that Vinteuil, in his latest works, seemed to have drawn nearer to that unknown country."[22]

Proust reaches a new profundity here when he links music to the sudden grace of involuntary memory. A revelatory aesthetics based in *anamnesis*, or unforgetting—every artist the bearer from another realm of some parcel of the lost fatherland, some moment of the forgotten festival—is allied to the novel's founding discovery, the vanished world restored by a madeleine and cup of linden tea: "Nothing resembled more closely than some such phrase of Vinteuil the peculiar pleasure which I had felt at certain moments in my life, when gazing, for instance, at the steeples of Martinville, or at certain trees along a road near Balbec, or, more simply at the beginning of this book, when I tasted a certain cup of tea. . . . One would have had to find, for the geranium scent of his music, not a material explanation, but the profound equivalent, the unknown, colorful festival (of which his works seemed to be the disconnected fragments, the scarlet-flashing splinters), the mode by which he 'heard' the universe and projected it far beyond himself. Perhaps it was in this, I said to Albertine, this unknown quality of a unique world which no other composer had ever yet revealed, that the most authentic proof of genius lies."[23]

* * *

The end of May brought another letter from Hauser, at the end of his rope with Proust's financial recklessness: "You live unfortunately in an atmosphere of idealism from which you certainly derive pleasures that are not easily available on earth. . . . You have grown up since your childhood, but you haven't aged, you have remained the child who does not allow himself to be scolded even when he is disobedient. This is why you have more or less eliminated from your circle all those who, refusing to succumb to your cajoling, have had the courage to scold you when you were being naughty. . . . I am quite happy to allow you to plunge body and soul into the Absolute, but only when you have paid back all your overdrafts."[24]

In the course of 1911 Proust had met, probably through Prince Constantin Radziwill, a shady character by the name of Albert Le Cuizat, afterward proprietor of a public bathhouse originally located near the Bourse and by 1915 in rue Godot-de-Mauroy, where it was known as the Bains du ballon d'Alsace. He had also opened a homosexual brothel at Hôtel Marigny, 11, rue de l'Arcade, which Proust may have helped him to acquire and to which he certainly did contribute some old furniture. According to Céleste Albaret, these pieces were intended for Albert's own quarters and Monsieur Proust was outraged to come upon them in the brothel.[25] But is it not more likely that he said this to spare her sense of propriety?

One evening, according to Céleste, Le Cuizat summoned Proust to Hôtel Marigny with the promise of something extraordinary: a wealthy industrialist from the north who came to Paris expressly to be chained and whipped by a young man till the two of them were drenched in blood. "Monsieur, how could you have watched that?" "Precisely because it cannot be invented, Céleste."[26]

It is clear that Proust would sometimes go to Hôtel Marigny as a customer, not just a researcher into the varieties of human nature. We now know from police records that on the night of January 11, 1918, he would be arrested at Le Cuizat's, along with the rest of the clientele, and booked as "Proust, Marcel, 46 years of age, of private income; address 102 bd Haussmann; drawn to pederasty."[27] Marcel Jouhandeau, also a patron of the Hôtel Marigny, reports in an unpublished notebook what one of the male prostitutes told him: that Proust would sometimes select a young man and ask him to stand across the room, undress, and masturbate while he, Proust, did the same in bed under a sheet. The prostitute reported to Jouhandeau that if Proust failed to satisfy himself by watching, the young man would be sent out and Le Cuizat would bring in a pair of cages containing two starving rats; the doors of the cages would be opened and the rats turned loose. Watching them tear at each other, Proust could finally achieve orgasm. This has been gloomily corroborated by additional sources—more and less reliable—including John Agate, Maurice Sachs, Count Boni de Castellane, Bernard Faÿ and others.[28] And Proust himself is perhaps hiding an admission of sorts in plain sight when, in *The Captive*, he gives, as his example of a nightmare, dead loved ones housed "in a little rat-cage."[29] Céleste would famously dispute all of these alleged oddities, saying of her employer's visits to Hôtel Marigny, "What interested him was the spectacle he'd seen, nothing else."[30] It is a view that has been unanimously mocked and dismissed by scholars.

On the subject of Proust's erotic tastes Tadié writes: "He required increasingly complicated scenarios: voyeurism and masturbation had always been at the wretched core of this. Proust possessed nothing and no one despite his attempts at relationships; the power he tried to exercise over people was of a moral kind, which explains the cross-examinations, the solemn pacts, the inevitability that to be loved by him was to stand trial. He never succeeded in these relationships except with his mother, and with Céleste Albaret. We should console ourselves with the thought that no historian has ever classified writers according to their sexual achievements."[31] All just and accurate and beyond anything said by earlier Proustians—though what is so wretched about voyeurism and masturbation I do not see. It's the *rats* we recoil from.

* * *

In May 1916 Proust revised the restaurant scene of *The Guermantes Way*, completed much earlier, to include a military conversation meant to be taking place at the height of the Dreyfus Affair. "The Kaiser is out for peace," declares a remarkably unprophetic Saint-Loup. "They're always making us think they want war, to force us to give in. Pure bluff, you know, like poker. . . . You have only to think what a cosmic thing a war would be today."[32] As the battle of Verdun raged on and on Proust drafted his sublime pages about wartime Paris for *Time Regained*, a historical account contemporaneous with events (by contrast to the *Search*'s depiction of the Affair, which was ex post facto). In a letter to Grasset, his soon-to-be ex-publisher, he wrote: "The conversations about military strategy have led me to make a connection at the end of the book, to introduce not the war as such but a few of its episodes, and M. de Charlus gets his due, incidentally, in this Paris bedecked with colorful soldiers reminiscent of a Carpaccio painting. There is nothing anti-militarist about any of this, needless to say; quite the reverse. But the newspapers are very foolish (and are treated extremely badly in my book)."[33]

In the trench warfare of Verdun 150,000 Frenchmen died; another 300,000 were mutilated. A beloved manservant at 102, boulevard Haussmann, Nicolas Cottin, had succumbed to pleurisy in an army hospital during the summer. "We are people in mourning who shall never rejoice again," Proust wrote Mme Straus at the close of 1916.[34]

Chapter Eleven

Some months earlier he had received from an admiring American in Paris, Walter Van Rensselaer Berry—lawyer, diplomatist, president of the American Chamber of Commerce in France, friend of Henry James and Edith Wharton—a rarity picked up in a secondhand book stall by the Seine: an eighteenth-century volume stamped with the arms and coronet of somebody named Pondre de Guermantes. This clever gift was the beginning of one of the most rewarding friendships of Proust's final years. Another of the brilliant younger men who came into his life at this time was Paul Morand, an attaché at the Ministry of Foreign Affairs and budding author who would be famous for his *Journal d'un attaché d'ambassade* among many other works—memoirs, short-story collections, and novels—and infamous for his collaborationist conduct in the Second World War. Morand had recently taken up with a cynosure of fashionable society, Princess Soutzo, *née* Hélène Chrissoveloni, Romanian, beautiful, and very rich, to whom Morand had introduced Proust over dinner at Larue's the previous spring. Proust liked her immediately and would frequently enjoy her lavish hospitality at the Ritz, Larue's, Ciro's, and the Crillon. (Morand was to marry his princess ten years later, and they would end their days together in the 1970s—among the last people to have known Marcel Proust—at her grand house in Avenue Charles-Floquet. Charles de Gaulle had a particular loathing for these two. Loyally *pétainiste*, they had served Vichy as ambassador and ambassadress to Bucharest from 1942 until Hitler's bombing of the city in August 1944 as the Red Army approached. For years de Gaulle did his utmost to keep Morand out of the Académie Française, but in 1968 the old collaborator finally did win the requisite number of votes.)

It was perhaps the spur of such new friendships that led Proust, despite asthma, angina, insomnia, and weakening eyesight, to go out more often in 1917, and not just on reconnaissance for his book. Three or more nights a week he would dine late on lobster and champagne at the Ritz, whether as the guest of Morand and Princess Soutzo, as host of a gathering, or on his own in a private room. The boys on staff were startlingly handsome and the dining room had a *premier maître d'hôtel*, Olivier Dabescat, who was richly informative about the restaurant's clientele and would abandon his duties to gossip with Proust for two and three hours at a time.

At one of the princess's supper parties Proust met the abbé of Sainte-Clothide, Arthur Mugnier.[1] A man of the world in a shabby cassock, sought after in high society for his wit, learning, and childlike charm, Mugnier worshiped the rarefied way of life of his aristocratic parishioners and would leave behind a journal spanning more than sixty years of Parisian high society (only a fraction of which has ever been published). At this dinner, the princess told Mugnier of a Jewish physician promulgating weird theories in Vienna about what dreams meant. Did

Proust overhear this? He had, in any case, propounded his own interpretation of dreams and nightmares in the as yet unpublished *Guermantes Way* and *Sodom and Gomorrah*. Quite unconcerned with catching out the repressed wishes Freud believed to be enciphered in dreams, Proust saw sleeping life more simply as the all-inclusive riverbed though which waking impressions flowed. He never read Freud and would have found the discoveries of psychoanalysis superfluous if he had.

* * *

Germany's resumption of unrestricted submarine warfare led to the sinking of six U.S. merchant ships in the early months of 1917. Wilhelm was trying to goad Woodrow Wilson into war. The breaking point came with American interception of a coded telegram from Arthur Zimmermann, German foreign secretary, bizarrely enticing Mexico to join the Central Powers on an empty promise of postwar assistance in the reconquest of Texas, Arizona, and New Mexico. On April 6 the United States entered the conflict.

Ten days later the Battle of the Chemin des Dames, advertised by General Robert Nivelle as a way of ending hostilities within forty-eight hours, began. Nivelle's offensive produced appalling casualties with derisory results. Reported in none of Proust's seven newspapers, or anywhere, was that on May 27, following a month of increasing desertions among French forces, thirty thousand men at Chemin des Dames, convinced of the strategic and tactical futility of their sacrifices, and convinced that their superiors did not understand the technological nature of the war being waged, left the front line and reserve trenches and went to the rear in a large-scale, organized mutiny that spread to include forty-nine divisions, just short of half the Frenchmen under arms. Nor did any paper report that on the eighth of June, 3,427 courts martial followed, after which between thirty and fifty of the leading mutineers were executed and about three thousand condemned to penal servitude. (Historian Guy Pedroncini revealed the extent of the insurrection only in 1967. Some military archives pertaining to the mutinies remain sealed until 2017.) But the mutineers had made their point; General Pétain ordered no more offensives till American tanks were at the front.[2]

Also in May the Germans introduced their Gotha bombers, far more destructive than the Zeppelins had been. After watching from the balcony of the Ritz as Gothas raided Le Bourget on the night of July 27—the first such aerial attack on metropolitan Paris since January of the previous year—Proust wrote a letter to Mme Straus describing what he'd seen, freely mingling the sublimity of Greco's *Burial of the Count of Orgaz* with Feydeau farce to make his point. The whole account seems a case of aesthetic wonder and comic delight trumping the horror: "I established myself on the Balcony and stayed for more than an hour in order to witness this admirable Apocalypse in which the bombers dove and rose, making and unmaking their constellations. If causing us to look at the sky had been all that happened, it would in itself have been beautiful, for the sky was so marvelous. What was unheard-of was that just as in Greco's painting where, above, you see the celestial scene and, below, the earthly one, so on the Balcony one saw the sublime fullness of the sky and, below, the Ritz. . . . Women in dressing gowns or even peignoirs prowled the halls, clutching at their pearls."[3]

In the course of 1917, at Proust's direction, Céleste burned thirty-two *cahiers* dating from before 1914. The introduction of the Albertine saga and the war theme had rendered obsolete his earlier conception of the novel's architecture. As he did not expect to live much longer and feared that certain of the early drafts might sow editorial confusion after his death, he wanted them destroyed.

* * *

On January 23, 1918, the Exposition Matisse-Picasso opened at Galerie Paul Guillaume, with catalogue copy by the great poet Apollinaire, wounded in the trenches two years earlier. Proust called the Matisse-Picasso exhibition, with his customary aptness of judgment in the fine arts, the most newsworthy spectacle of the moment. News of another sort broke one week later, when newly Bolshevist Russia sued for peace with the Central Powers and left the war. The Triple Alliance was no more. On the evening of that day, beginning at 11:30 P.M., Gotha bombers dropped 267 devices on Paris, killing sixty-five and wounding nearly two hundred. Returning home by taxi from a musical performance at Gabriel La Rochefoucauld's, Proust heard the sirens. He stepped out onto avenue de Messine for a better view of the attack. In nearby rue d'Athènes there was a direct hit.

That night was to be the first of almost daily aerial attacks on the capital for the next three months. Alone of the residents at 102, boulevard Haussmann, Proust always refused to descend from the "empyrean to the depths"—that is, take shelter in the basement during bombardments. As well, he declined Mme Catusse's offer of her villa on Mont Boron at Nice, bitterly disappointing Céleste, who was dreaming of southern suns. Her employer would die without ever seeing the south of France. Parisian he remained, and socially active in 1917 despite the shelling. On February 4 he attended a dinner at Mme Daudet's in honor of Francis Jammes and met the extraordinary young novelist François Mauriac, an important friend for the rest of his life.[4]

The following month came aerial attacks that could not be aesthetically regarded. On March 8 Gothas dropped ninety bombs, prompting an exodus to the countryside by more than 200,000. And in the early morning of March 23 so-called Big Berthas, long-range canon wheeled into position at Crépy-en-Laonnois, shelled the city, killing 256 civilians. Then on the twenty-ninth, Good Friday, at 4:30 P.M., a Bertha shell hit the church of Saint-Gervais-et-Saint-Protais in the Marais, killing seventy-five and wounding ninety of those assembled for Tenebrae, the Good Friday evening service in which all tapers but one are extinguished and the single remaining flame is hidden beneath the altar. In a letter to Jacques Truelle, Proust would compare the war to Tenebrae and its hidden flame: "I have faith in the glimmer of light, but I don't know where it will come from."[5]

He was struggling with new physical symptoms—mild aphasia and a facial paralysis that may have been Bell's palsy. The bright spot in early April was a visit—unexpected and overwhelming—by his brother, on leave from the southern front near Padua, to which he'd been dispatched as commander of an ambulance unit after the Italian defeat at Isonzo. On the bedside table Robert would probably have noticed and rejoiced in page proofs of *In the Shadow of Young Girls in Flower*, newly arrived from NRF—volume two of the five-volume work Proust and his publisher were now projecting.

French, British, and American forces recaptured Soissons on May 29 with heavy losses. The bombings of Paris had ceased, but no one knew when they might resume. In drafts of the *Search* as well as in letters, Proust likened the capital under fire to Pompeii, as when he wrote on June 24 to Étienne de Beaumont: "Women getting ready to dine in town may find themselves interrupted and delayed forever, on the point of departure, just as they are applying the last touch of powder to their cheeks, halted by flying Vesuvian lava from the Boches; all those fancy goods, now rendered august and immutable, will be used for the instruction of children in the schools of a better age."[6] He had learned, after four years of war, to say "Boche" like everyone else.

At the Ritz there were a number of memorable sightings. One evening that summer Proust observed at the next table Great Britain's minister of munitions, Winston Churchill, among his entourage. The Ritz staff had much to offer, too. Beginning sometime that spring Proust was in contact with one waiter in particular, a good-looking Swiss named Henri Rochat. That Proust would sometimes procure young men—teenagers, in fact—from the hotel staff is well established. His lavish tips were a signal to them of what was wanted. Sixty years later Camille Wixler, another Swiss and one of Rochat's coworkers, explained to an interviewer: "At that age, my education did not permit me to imagine what was going on, but afterwards I discovered from Monsieur Proust himself what it was all about. He gave me to understand that certain kinds of human beings were not made as others were."[7] Proust promised young Camille that his name would be included in the *Search;* and indeed, a servant of the Swann household is named Camille in *In the Shadow of Young Girls in Flower.*

The likely pretext was that having dined late, a gentleman would ask for assistance getting home and up the stairs. Thus, while Céleste and the rest of the household slept at their end of the flat, a young man might accompany Proust to his room. Or else a prior arrangement would have been made and the young man would present himself late in the evening. Determined to hear and see nothing, Céleste heard and saw nothing.

In the case of Rochat, Proust's favorite among the youths of the Ritz, the infatuation was expensive. A letter to Hauser of September 15 tacitly referred to him as follows: "When one is in love with a person from the working class, more or less, rather than someone in society, these heartaches are generally coupled with considerable financial difficulties."[8] By the turn of the year Rochat would gain the title of "secretary" at boulevard Haussmann and move in, no doubt to Céleste's immeasurable disgust. He played solitaire, painted, took a bit of dictation—and cadged large sums from his love-struck employer.

* * *

French, English, Australian, and Canadian troops launched a sudden and savage offensive east of Amiens on August 8, 1918, gaining eight miles of ground and killing, wounding, or capturing nearly thirty thousand of an enemy that, having lost more than a million men since March, was coming to the end of its capacity to fight. Amiens marked the start of the so-called Hundred Days Offensive that would lead to German capitulation in November. A failure to keep technological pace with Allied war manufacturing had put Germany at a fatal disadvantage in the field. Allied command under Marshall Foch remained shrewdly coordinated, while Ludendorff, his opposite number, veered in confusion. Meanwhile, as German morale collapsed, a quarter of a million Americans arrived every month. Whole groups of exhausted Germans were surrendering to individual Allied soldiers. Among Austro-Hungarian forces more than 300,000 had deserted. In mid-September the new emperor, Karl, Franz Josef's great nephew, proposed cessation of hostilities without prior conditions, an offer contemptuously refused by the Allies, for whom unconditional surrender of all the Central Powers was now a feasible goal.

Bulgaria was first to sue for peace. When Ludendorff heard the news on September 27 he fell to the floor and foamed at the mouth. And, in a major strategic gain, Allied forces broke through the Hindenburg Line at Saint-Quentin Canal. Convening the high command at his headquarters in Spa, Ludendorff announced bluntly, and to general amazement, that the war was lost. On October 6 the Germans abandoned the ruin they had made of Reims; the following week French forces drove them from Laon, occupied since the start of the war. On November 6, in a railway car in the Forest of Compiègne, Ferdinand Foch presented unconditional terms to Matthias Erzberger, the German government's envoy. Three days after that, back in Berlin, Kaiser Wilhelm lost the support of his generals and was forced to abdicate and go into exile. Erzberger, who'd begun the Compiègne negotiations on behalf of a monarchy, now concluded them in the name of a republic born in defeat and threatened by communist revolution. At the eleventh hour of the eleventh day of the eleventh month of 1918, amid a universal ringing of bells, the bloodiest European war was over.

* * *

On the winning side old energies revived. Unscathed somehow by his years at the front, Reynaldo was quickly back in Paris and conducting at the Opéra-Comique. The publishing industry came back to life; Proust and NRF now projected six volumes for the *Search*.

Near the end of 1918 the Comtesse Adhéaume de Chevigné, one of Proust's long-meditated "keys" for Oriane de Guermantes—"the hooked nose of a bird, the piercing, soft eyes, the white-gloved arm leaning on a box at the theatre," as he'd depicted her back in 1892—consented to dine with him at the Ritz. She was an old sly boots, fully aware of the convenience Proust was making of her in his book and aristocratically skeptical of the motives of a jumped-up little bourgeois. But skepticism was returned in kind, and with interest, in the volumes to come. The Narrator's nearer contact with the Faubourg—epitomized in the *Search* by Mme de Guermantes—is a school of disillusionment. Our hero cannot, as Tadié observes, "be admitted into the realm of the Duchesse unless, like Alberich in *Das Rheingold*, he renounces his love for her; and, in order to mix in society, he no longer writes. But the punishment is more severe still: to have access to the Guermantes is to dispel the poetry evoked by their names; people's names are just like place-names, and life always refutes dreams."[9] Proust had written many letters to Mme de Chevigné over the years. Her opinion of *In Search of Lost Time* may be judged from the bonfire she made of them after his death.

Alongside the man-made calamity of world war there was nature's own, the influenza epidemic of 1918, claiming perhaps five times as many lives as the hostilities. In July, following a serious case of the disease, Céleste convalesced in Lozère for two weeks with her family, leaving her sister-in-law Adèle Larivière to cope as she could with Monsieur Proust's imperious and unpredictable demands. Promptly at the end of the two weeks Céleste was back at her duties, though she now needed help. By November her elder sister, Marie Gineste, had come to live in boulevard Haussmann.

One January evening, upon returning from a dinner at the Ritz with Walter Berry at which he found himself unable to speak on account of asthma, Proust found a devastating letter from his great Aunt Amélie Weil, Uncle Louis's widow, who very calmly informed him that she had sold 102, boulevard Haussmann to the Banque Varin-Bernier. He'd never had a lease with her, only a familial understanding, which now turned out to be no understanding at all. In a letter to Berry, he wrote that "for an asthmatic, moving house tends to be fatal,"[10] and the weeks and months that followed Aunt Amélie's announcement were a torment of breathlessness, sleeplessness, angina, slurred speech, worsening eyestrain—and bafflement as to where he would live. The extent of this calamity may perhaps be judged by an entry in the diary of the British diplomat and author Harold Nicholson, who'd dined with Proust at the invitation of Princess Soutzo that spring: "pale, unshaven and dirty, with a face like papier-mâché," Nicholson noted; and "very Hebrew,"[11]—which was true. People more and more saw in him the Old Testament prophet. Like Swann as he declines, Proust had the look of someone living on locusts and wild honey.

In April, Jacques Rivière, who'd been taken captive at the first Battle of the Marne, published *Germany: Memories and Reflections of a Prisoner of War*, read by Proust with the greatest admiration. Rivière had been, at the outbreak, Jacques Copeau's second in command at the *Nouvelle Revue Française* and would take over operations after the war, naming Jean Paulhan his own second. A letter to Rivière, whom Proust considered his best reader, reveals the *Search*'s method of slow revelation, everything the reader thinks he knows giving way to a wisdom hitherto unimaginable: "I thought it more honorable and tactful as an artist not to let it be seen, not to proclaim that I was setting out precisely in search of the Truth, nor to say what it consisted in for me. I so hate those ideological works in which the novel is a constant betrayal of the author's intentions that I preferred to say nothing. It's only at the end of the book, when the lessons of life have been grasped, that my design will become clear."[12]

On April 19, 1919, having read the proofs of *In the Shadow of Young Girls in Flower*, Rivière asked to run an excerpt at the front of an issue relaunching the *Revue*. And in mid-April Sydney Schiff, editor of *Arts and Letters* in London, also asked for an extract. (Schiff was himself a novelist who wrote under the name Stephen Hudson.) Thus began Proust's friendship with him and his wife, Violet, which would develop quickly and rewardingly.

The struggle to read four thousand pages of proofs was exhausting and enraging. On May 22 Proust exploded, cursing Gaston Gallimard for delays followed by too many sheets all at once, and for the too-small typeface in which *In the Shadow of Young Girls in Flower* had been set. Like many writers in the months before publication, Proust saw the smiling face of doom wherever he turned. And there was, to further torment him, the impending move. It was at this moment that he sold most of his possessions. What he chiefly took to temporary lodgings—apart from the tenacious and now unloved Henri Rochat—were his brass bed, tarnished by years of Legras-powder fumigations, his Chinese cabinet, three little tables, the green-glass lamp, and other items to be seen today in Proust's reconstructed bedroom at the Musée Carnavalet in Paris. On May 30 a bewildered and desolate Marcel made his move to the fourth floor at 8 *bis*, rue Laurent-Pichat, between avenue

Foch and rue Pergolèse, owned by the celebrated actress Réjane, who lived on the second floor. Her son, Jacques Porel, gassed in the war and now a semi-invalid, lived with a wife and child on the third. Réjane's performance in *Germinie Lacerteux* at the Odéon thirty years earlier had produced in young Marcel a "recurrent fever," he declared in an inscription to her. She had been the chief model for La Berma, one of the great artists of the *Search*, as she doubtless knew.

At last, on June 21, 1919, Gallimard brought out *In the Shadow of Young Girls in Flower*, *Pastiches and Mélanges*, and the new edition of *Swann's Way*. The last differed in one notable respect from Grasset's 1913 version: Combray, and nearby Roussainville and Méseglie, previously in the vicinity of Chartres, have migrated eastward to somewhere between Laon and Rheims—in other words, into the line of the German advance. This emendation of volume one would pay dividends in volume seven, where Mme de Forcheville (Gilberte) describes the fictive eight-month "Battle of Méséglise" with its destruction of the local church and ravaging of the countryside. "Probably, like me," she writes to the Narrator, "you did not imagine that obscure Roussainville and boring Méséglise, where our letters used to be brought from and where the doctor was once fetched when you were ill, would ever be famous places. Well, my dear friend, they have become forever a part of history, with the same claim to glory as Austerlitz or Valmy. The battle of Méséglise lasted for more than eight months; the Germans lost in it more than six hundred thousand men, they destroyed Méséglise, but they did not capture it. As for the short cut up the hill, which you were so fond of and which we used to call the hawthorn path, where you claim that as a small child you fell in love with me (whereas I assure you in all truthfulness that it was I who was in love with you), I cannot tell you how important it has become. The huge field of corn upon which it emerges is the famous Hill 307, which you must have seen mentioned again and again in the bulletins. The French blew up the little bridge over the Vivonne that you said did not remind you of your childhood as much as you would have wished, and the Germans have thrown other bridges across the river. For a year and a half they held one half of Combray and the French the other."[13]

On June 28 the peace treaty ending the Great War was signed at Versailles, five years to the day after Gavrilo Prizip murdered Archduke Francis Ferdinand and his wife at Sarajevo. Of the pauperizing and retributive peace imposed on Germany by the victors, Marshal Foch spoke that day as a prophet. "This is not peace," he famously said. "It is an armistice for twenty years." Twenty years and sixty-eight days later a second world war, greater by orders of magnitude than the first, would engulf humanity.

That summer Proust saw his first royalties in many years, income badly needed owing to the extravagant expenditures on Rochat. The young man, suffering from gonorrhea after a stay on the Riviera, now decided to return to Switzerland. Proust saw him onto a train at Gare de Lyon—to be certain the boy went?—and afterward hosted Walter Berry, Mme Soutzo, and Paul Morand for supper at the Ritz. There was much to celebrate. He believed he was rid of Rochat.

Chapter Twelve

In a splendid letter to his new friends Violet and Sydney Schiff, who'd been in touch that summer after reading *In the Shadow of Young Girls in Flower*, Proust said he too regretted that Swann, following his marriage to Odette, becomes so much less appealing. But it must be so, Proust told them: "Art is a perpetual sacrifice of sentiment to truth." Like them he was a friend to Swann—but a greater friend to truth: "*Amicus Swann sed magna amicus veritas.*"[1]

The truth of Charles Swann, as of Proust's whole cast of characters, is not in a first view but in the metamorphoses time discloses. Proust's novel is immensely long because it must be in order to accommodate so many gradual transformations. He hastened to assure the Schiffs that, before dying, Swann—magnificently, fearlessly Dreyfusard—will have redeemed himself. "It is as difficult," Proust says in *The Captive*, "to present a fixed image of a character as of societies and passions. For a character alters no less than they do, and if one tries to take a snapshot of what is relatively immutable in it, one finds it presenting a succession of different aspects (implying that it is incapable of keeping still but keeps moving) to the disconcerted lens."[2]

Also dating from this moment is a funny, poignant, astoundingly frank yet very mysterious letter to Jacques Porel, to whom Proust had taken a strong liking: "The neighbors who are separated from me by a partition make . . . love every day with a frenzy that makes me jealous. . . . On first hearing them I thought a murder was taking place, although very soon the woman's cry, which was repeated an octave lower by the man, made me realize what was going on. . . . No sooner is the last cry achieved then they rush off to take a Sitz bath, their murmurs fading into the sound of water. The complete absence of any transition exhausts me on their behalf, for if there is anything I loathe *afterward*, or at least *immediately afterward*, it is having to move. Whatever the selfishness of preserving the warmth of a mouth that has nothing more to receive."[3]

What to make of this? It would promptly contribute to the noisy lovemaking of Charlus and Jupien in the prologue to *Sodom and Gomorrah* and of the bathing afterward. But "preserving the warmth of a mouth that has nothing more to receive"? Boys from the Ritz obliged him to this extent? Very doubtful. In this strange letter he is enjoying the pleasure of being assumed to be heterosexual, boasting to Porel, who did not know him well, of imaginary exploits.

Proust ended his temporary stay in rue Laurent-Pichat on October 1 with the move to an apartment on the fifth floor of 44, rue Hamelin, near the Étoile. Céleste, Odilon, and Marie Gineste were with him—and Rochat, that bad penny, back from Switzerland.

Reviews of *In the Shadow of Young Girls in Flower* came in mixed. A young Louis Aragon wrote in the October number of

Littérature: "Eventually one marvels, when Marcel Proust does a pastiche of Marcel Proust, at finding so little brilliance in someone who displays such talent. To tell the truth, my digestion cannot cope with miscellanies." Not Aragon's most shining hour. Adding to the affronts, Morand later that month published a poem called "Ode to Marcel Proust" which suggested the great novelist must be, in the off-hours, a visitor to louche locations; no more than the truth, though most unwelcome in print, however veiled; Proust had the recent memory of being arrested at Le Cuizat's brothel. Morand's ode briefly strained the bonds, though not to breaking—as with poor old Lionel Hauser, who that autumn could take no more of Proust's profligacy and resigned in disgust as his financial adviser. Yet another blow.

On December 10 the Prix Goncourt, France's highest literary honor, was awarded to *In the Shadow of Young Girls in Flower.* The runner-up was Roland Dorgelès's *Les Croix de bois,* a war novel for which there had been patriotic and middlebrow support. Considerable public debate followed the jury's decision. "Make way for the old!" declared *L'Humanité,* the communist paper. And Noel Garnier wrote in *Le Populaire:* "We soldiers voted for Dorgelès. Marcel Proust owes his prize to the recognition of six men whom he took out to dinner." On New Year's Day, 1920, a formidable piece by Rivière in the *Nouvelle Revue Française* effectively ended the controversy: "The Académie Goncourt's choice, despite having displeased certain journalists, will most assuredly be ratified by the next generation. What better proof of the justness of the award?" He followed up, a month later, with "Marcel Proust et la tradition classique," where he wrote: "Only masterpieces have the privilege of facing down, upon their appearance in the world, an orchestrated chorus of enemies. Such imbeciles never revolt except when they feel injured."[4]

An originality remaking the traditions of literature and furnishing an entirely new vision had proved, not surprisingly, too much for some to bear. Such was Proust's view of his own achievement: to have transformed the French language itself by force of a comprehensive new grasp of life. Ordinarily gifted novelists leave language and theme as they find them. The very greatest are, by contrast, a kind of catastrophe; everything is understood anew in their wake. Proust's "À propos du 'style' de Flaubert" ran in the same number of the *Nouvelle Revue Française* as Rivière's defense of the *Search.* Writing of Flaubert's revolution, Proust was simultaneously describing his own: "A man who through his utterly new and personal use of the preterite and past indefinite tenses, of the present participle, and certain pronouns and prepositions, has renewed our vision as much as Kant, with his Categories, and his theories of Knowledge and the Reality of the exterior world."[5]

He now embarked on a hapless campaign to get himself elected to the Académie Française—appearing unannounced late one evening, for example, at the door of an outraged Maurice Barrès, no admirer to begin with. Bleary-eyed, unshaven, wrapped in an enormous muffler, Proust cut a pathetic figure on Barrès's doorstep. He had long ago dreamed of making his father proud by standing among the *Immortels.* In addition to Barrès, those currently holding chairs included Paul Bourget, Henri Bergson, Marshal Foch, General Joffre, Henri de Régnier, and Anatole France (with whom Proust hadn't communicated in many years). Not, by and large, a group likely to rally to *In Search of Lost Time,* though two or three probably would have. Rivière considered the Académie irrelevant and consoled Proust by saying of Barrès and the others that they "cannot understand you; their slumber is too deep."[6] Indeed; when has the opinion of Quai de Conti's alleged immortals ever mattered, finally? In September, after reading proofs of *The Guermantes Way,* Lucien Daudet arrived at the proper judgment of Proust's worth: "You have re-created the novel, and you are the greatest novelist who has ever lived in any epoch in any country. Because you have everything that all the others had and, in addition, everything that is yours."[7]

Also in September Proust roused himself to attend an afternoon meeting of the Blumenthal Prize committee, charged with awarding its substantial purse to a young author of exceptional merit. Proust spoke in favor of Rivière for the award and gained unanimous consent from his fellow jurors, who included Gide, Valéry, Bergson, Robert de Flers, Comtesse de Noailles, the ever-indignant Barrès (even he was won over), and several others. One committee member, René Boylesve, recalled Proust thus: "Flesh that was blue, like the color of high game. . . . Despite the moustache, he had the look of a sixty-year-old Jewish lady who might have been beautiful. His eyes, in profile, were oriental."[8]

In these months he was actively preparing people—reviewers particularly—for the homosexual content of *Sodom and Gomorrah*, volume four of the *Search*. What was previously in hieroglyph would now be made plain. In October he wrote warningly to critic Paul Souday, who'd long ago panned *Swann's Way*, that the plot was going to "take a bad turn through no fault of mine. My characters don't turn out well; I must follow them where their serious defects or vices lead me."[9] Such attempts to shape the critical response turn up with increasing frequency in his correspondence. Near the end of the year, in a characteristic letter to Louis Martin Chauffier at the *Nouvelle Revue Françiase*, he all but gave instructions that their reviewer should "make it very clear that *The Guermantes Way* is the exact opposite of a snobbish book. . . . The truth is that by natural logic after having confronted the poetry of the name Balbec with the triviality of the place Balbec, I had to proceed in the same manner for the proper name Guermantes." And there is this from the same letter, his deepest hint to date about the *Search* as a whole: "The only thing I don't say about the

Narrator is that at the end he is a writer, because the entire book could be called a vocation . . . but which is not discovered until the last volume."[10]

With *The Guermantes Way* newly arrived in bookshops and selling briskly, Proust was on November 7 made an officer of the Légion d'Honneur for his services to France; but as he was not well enough for a public ceremony, Robert Proust, promoted already to the rank of *officier* for his wartime heroism, was deputed to 44, rue Hamelin to place the red ribbon and diamond-studded cross around his brother's neck. He stayed to dine at the bedside. They spoke of their parents late into the night.[11]

* * *

On New Year's Day, 1921, the *Nouvelle Revue* published "An Agony," the scene from *The Guermantes Way* in which Grand'mère dies. Three weeks later the *Revue hebdomadaire* published, with brief introductory remarks by Mauriac, "A Night of Fog," another excerpt from the new volume, in which the Narrator speaks prophetically of "the detour of many wasted years through which I was yet to pass before the invisible vocation of which this book is the history declared itself."[12] In his preface Mauriac named Proust likeliest of all living authors to achieve immortality—the real kind, not what the Institut de France bestows—and praised the *Search*, or what he knew of it at this time, as a "summa of contemporary sensitivity"[13]—that unwelcome word again. In the *Nouvelle Revue* Gide published "Billet à Angèle," his heartfelt and magnificent praise of Proust as a greater writer than himself, calling the style "so disconcerting in its suppleness that any other style appears stilted, dull, imprecise, sketchy, lifeless. Should I admit that when I plunge again into this lake of delights, for many days afterward I remain afraid to pick up the pen, no longer believing myself capable—as happens during the time a masterpiece holds us in its sway—of writing well, seeing in what is called the 'purity' of my style only 'poverty.' "[14]

Gide would change his tune when he read the soon to be published next volume, *Sodom and Gomorrah*, whose depiction of homosexuality he loathed. In lieu of Proust's wretched and secretive men, Gide was dreaming of a breed of joyously masculine homosexuals on the ancient Greek model. Not even Saint-Loup, as yet unrevealed to readers in his true complexity, was going to satisfy Gide's requirements: Saint-Loup, malest of males, handsome, brave—and queer, madly in love with the elevator boy at Balbec while carrying on his tempestuous affair with the actress Rachel; madly in love, later, with the beautiful and hideous Morel.

Mauriac too was going to recoil from *Sodom and Gomorrah*, though not for Gide's reasons. Mauriac's homosexuality was and would remain unavowed, a torment branching deep beneath the surface of seventy books. Tadié sketches him brilliantly: "Mauriac's secret was much the same as Proust's, and the man whose life was filled with earthly joys, and later with honors, was no more at peace, nor perhaps any happier, than the great solitary invalid. Proust would not influence Mauriac's novels, but for the author of *Un Adolescent d'autrefois* right up to the superb pages of *Mémoires* and *Nouveaux mémoires interieurs*, he would continue to be a constant reference point, rather like a guardian angel, one finger raised to his lips."[15] Mauriac wrote to Proust on March 1, after dining in rue Hamelin: "You are the only person I admire effortlessly and without any ulterior motive. . . . I enter the enchantment of your books just as I did as a child those of Jules Verne and Féval."[16] But in the *Journal of a Thirty-Year-Old*, set down in 1924, his depiction of the evening was more clinical: "A curious supper . . . at ten o'clock at night at Proust's bedside: sheets none too clean, the stench of the furnished flat, his Jewish features, with his ten-day growth of beard, sinking back into ancestral filth. A subject resumed in his books."[17] Mauriac is surely thinking of the famous passage in *Sodom and Gomorrah* about how Jewish the dying Swann has come to look.

On May 2 the second half of *The Guermantes Way* and the first half of *Sodom and Gomorrah* appeared as one volume in the bookshops. Proust inscribed Céleste's copy as follows: "To my faithful friend of eight years, but in reality so united with my thoughts that I would be closer to the truth in calling her my friend of always, not being able to imagine a time when I did not know her. . . . To Céleste the War Cross, because she tolerated Gothas and Berthas; to Céleste who has borne the cross of my temperament; to Céleste the Cross of Honor, Her friend Marcel."[18] Angry responses to the book were soon to reach Proust's ears: Comtesse de Chevigné predictably saw herself in Oriane de Guermantes; Louis d'Albufera saw himself in Saint-Loup; Robert de Montesquiou saw himself in Charlus. Had these people not understood for whom they were posing? Had they imagined Marcel was only enjoying their company, not strip-mining them for the ore they contained? Did they not know that this is what novelists do?

Later that month Gide paid a call to rue Hamelin and left the typescript of *Corydon*, his unpublished dialogues on man-boy love, which he asked Proust to read under seal of secrecy. Four evenings later Gide returned and the two talked through the night, in the course of which Proust said that all his life he had exclusively desired men, loving women only "spirituellement."[19] Gide confided this within hours to his diary and we may take it as settling the matter of Proust's sexuality. Androgynous in his work, like all the greatest novelists—yes, by all means. Bisexual, never.

* * *

"I went out . . . in a state to make one believe that my death might well be a brief news item the following day, among all the dogs that had been run over," Proust reports in late May to Étienne de Beaumont.[20] This daytime outing was to an exhibition of Dutch art at the Jeu de Paume where "the most beautiful painting in the world"—Vermeer's *View of Delft*, with its little patch of yellow wall, last seen by him in The Hague almost twenty years earlier—was on view.

Did he fall ill while there? It seems he may have. Such, in any case, will be the circumstance in which Bergotte suddenly dies in *The Captive*, a scene planned before Proust went to the Jeu de Paume but expanded and no doubt altered with fresh details afterward: Bergotte "repeated to himself: 'Little patch of yellow wall, with a sloping roof, little patch of yellow wall.' Meanwhile he sank down onto a circular settee; whereupon he suddenly ceased to think that his life was in jeopardy and, reverting to his natural optimism, told himself: 'It's nothing, merely a touch of indigestion from those potatoes, which were undercooked.' A fresh attack struck him down; he rolled from the settee to the floor, as visitors and attendants came hurrying to his assistance. He was dead. Dead forever? Who can say?"[21] A photo of Proust snapped outside the exhibition that day would be the last until the one Man Ray took at the deathbed. In it he wears a swallowtail coat and striped trousers, holds a walking stick and hat, and looks remarkably well, jaunty even, despite deep shadows under the eyes.

Henri Rochat finally left the rue Hamelin household for good in June, immigrating to Buenos Aires, where Horace Finaly had kindly secured a position for him in a bank. There is no record of the young man after this date; Rochat disappeared into the long grass. Meanwhile Gaston Gallimard had become another sort of burden, now deeply in arrears with royalties to Proust, his most important author. Fifty thousand francs were owed, money badly needed in the wake of Rochat.

Early July brought a letter from one of Proust's greatest French contemporaries, Colette, who was beside herself after reading *Sodom and Gomorrah:* "No one in the world has written pages such as these on homosexuals, no one!"[22] Mauriac was accountably more solemn: "Impossible for you not to bear this terrible fruit. It had to fall to you and not to another to assume the role of angel who makes the accursed cities rise from their ashes."[23] The fat was in the fire, Proust having put his forbidden subject matter before the public. On August 28, in a letter to Charles Maurras, he contrasted ancient and modern homosexuality: "In those times, these propensities, which were very often a reflection of passion, of the desire to be like others, were natural. So many centuries of disapproval have meant that they are only allowed to survive among the sick who are powerless to cure them. And this is why in my books I appear to be blaming something I do not condemn, as I continue joylessly through the valleys with their stench of pitch and sulphur."[24] In pursuit of this stench, Proust's chief predecessor had been the Balzac who created Vautrin in *Old Goriot*, *Lost Illusions*, and *Splendors and Miseries of Courtesans.* But how much farther *Sodom and Gomorrah* goes! A letter in October from Rivière hailed Proust as the "creator of a society as complete and complex as that of the *Comédie humaine.* You have the additional merit over Balzac of not having just presented and described it, but explored and explained."[25]

Also that autumn there arrived a letter from Bernard Faÿ—hero of Verdun, professor at both the Collège de France and Columbia University in New York where he taught French literature each spring term. (Faÿ would later be the translator of Gertrude Stein and protector of her and Alice Toklas during the Nazi Occupation, throughout which he headed the Bibliothèque Nationale. Following the Liberation he was sentenced to hard labor for life as a collaborator, a punishment from which he escaped in 1951 to Fribourg, Switzerland, till amnestied in 1959.)[26] Faÿ wished to speak with Proust about how to present *Swann's Way*, *In the Shadow of Young Girls in Flower*, *The Guer-*

mantes Way, and *Sodom and Gomorrah* at Columbia and how to direct dissertations on them. Proust received him for dinner at his bedside.

Meanwhile Ezra Pound had published "Saint-Loup: A Portrait," excerpted from *The Guermantes Way*, in *The Dial*. And, momentously, Charles Kenneth Scott Moncrieff had announced plans to translate the whole cycle. (Scott Moncrieff promptly got a letter from Edmund Gosse urging him to reconsider, as Proust was an insignificant writer with little chance of being remembered.)[27] And there had come this from an American woman, twenty-seven and very beautiful by her own account, who said she'd been reading Proust night and day for three years: "Dear Marcel Proust, Quit being such a poseur. Come down for once from your empyrean and tell me in two lines what you meant to say." "I reckoned there was no point in replying to her," Proust told Walter Berry.[28]

December 11, 1921, brought a shock—the death at Menton of Robert de Montesquiou from untreated uremia—though along with Proust's very real sadness there was anxiety about how he might figure in the count's posthumous memoirs. He needn't have worried. Apart from a handful of Proust scholars, nobody has ever read *Les Pas effacés*, in which Proust is indeed called "mendacious."

Had reading the portrait of Charlus in the early pages of *Sodom and Gomorrah* killed Montesquiou? Tadié says no, but I tend to think it gave just the required nudge. In any case Proust was being more than a little naughty when, in a letter of condolence on December 18 to the Duchesse de Guiche, he described her kinsman Montesquiou as "a man he could have written volumes about." He already had.[29]

That New Year's Eve—Proust's last—was celebrated festively all night at the palatial residence of the Comte and Comtesse de Beaumont. Picasso too was present, and in *Le Regard de la mémoire* Jean Hugo recalls him saying of Proust: "Look, he's keeping his eye out for models."[30] Well, no. The *Search* was all but done. There would be no new venture; Marcel knew that death had set a watch on him. In his introduction to *Tendres stocks*, Morand's wretchedly entitled collection of three novels, Proust wrote: "A strange woman has chosen to make her home in my brain."[31] We'll encounter her again as the witch lurking round his deathbed, the woman in black whom no one can touch.

* * *

He attended his niece Suzy's eighteenth birthday party on January 28 at Robert and Marthe's house, where he'd very rarely been over the years. "All told, my presence did not cast the chill of the resurrection of Lazarus too much," he wrote afterward to Morand. "It is true that I'm going back to the tomb."[32] Five days later—on the day, as it happened, that Sylvia Beach published Joyce's *Ulysses* at Shakespeare & Co.—Proust wrote to the Duchesse de Clermont-Tonnerre that no letters from him should be preserved, much less published. But after all, what in his surviving correspondence is intimate, beyond the letter to Porel and perhaps a few others dating from adolescence? Most of the love letters of Proust's manhood—and there must have been many—have gone missing, have been destroyed, or are withheld from scholarly inspection: to Edgar Aubert, Willie Heath, Reynaldo (five years' of which are missing); to Lucien (letters that exist in a private collection but remain out of reach), Bertrand, and Alfred (save the sole surviving document already mentioned). Proust in love is a man who must be inferred rather than known directly. At any rate, there is evidence about a final attachment in late 1921 or early 1922. Proust took to a very young waiter surnamed Vanelli (Christian name unknown) at the Ritz and arranged, through Camille Wixler, for the boy to serve him coffee after dinner. According to Wixler's much later testimony, Proust also took Vanelli home to rue Hamelin.

Along with his asthma fumigations, he'd grown increasingly reliant on digitalis and Veronal. The abuse of the latter, a barbiturate, dated back more than twenty years and had worsened dangerously. Particularly frightening to Céleste was his loss of appetite. And yet the immense volume of incoming mail somehow got answered. In March Proust responded to critic Camille Vettard's queries with the following metaphor for his art: "a telescope fixed upon time" permitting phenomena utterly forgotten and situated far back in the past to appear to consciousness.[33]

At the end of April an excerpt from *Sodom and Gomorrah* entitled "An evening with the Verdurins" appeared in *Les Feuilles libres*. At some point in the course of the spring, not specifiable, Proust called Céleste to his room and, beaming like a child in bed, told her: "I have important news. Tonight I wrote the word 'fin.' . . . Now I can die."[34]

On May 1 he took an accidental overdose of dry adrenaline before going to the Ritz with Violet and Sydney. Upon returning home his condition worsened into weeks of recurring fever and inability to eat. His digestive tract had been severely burned, and from this date Proust consumed little else than ice cream and iced beer brought home by Odilon from the Ritz. It was not until May 18 that he ventured out again, to a supper party hosted by Violet and Sydney at the Hôtel Majestic following the premiere of *Renard*, Stravinsky's new ballet. Present were the Stravinskys, the Picassos, Diaghilev—and James Joyce, in the wrong clothes and drinking too much. Many variants of what the authors of *Ulysses* and *In Search of Lost Time* said to each other that evening survive, owing to Joyce's penchant for telling the story differently each time; whereas Proust, who could make nothing of the greatest living novelist in the English language, never mentioned the meeting to anyone. After awkward civilities Proust seems to have asked Joyce's opinion of truffles, and Joyce allowed as he liked them, and so on, miserably. One thing was clear: These mighty opposites had no wish to meet again.

Now Proust received a vituperative letter ("monstre," and so on) from Laure Hayman, who'd recognized herself in the figure of Odette de Crécy.[35] But why only now? *Swann's Way* had been in print for nine years. Proust gave her the usual self-exculpatory song and dance, then bade her farewell, but not before paraphrasing one of the gems of *Sodom and Gomorrah:* "People in society are too apt to think of a book as a sort of cube one side of which can be removed, so that the author can at once 'put in' the people he meets."[36] But there was no explaining to Laure Hayman her good luck—that so far from being merely "put in," she was apotheosized and made deathless on the page. No, Laure liked coming upon herself in a novel no better than most people do.

* * *

Near the end of the month, shortly before the Schiffs returned to London, Proust took Sydney to Le Cuizat's brothel. Did he believe that he and Sydney shared those tastes? Unlikely. Proust afterward apologized for having put him through the experience. What happened at Hôtel Marigny is unknown and there is absolutely no evidence that Sydney was homosexual. But could Proust have been offering a preview of one of the important settings of *Time Regained*—a book Sydney knew nothing of yet but was destined to translate after Scott Moncrieff's death?

At what was to prove their final meeting, on June 4, Lucien Daudet was horrified by his old friend's spectral appearance. However impeded by the great name of Daudet, Lucien had managed, before the war, to publish a well-regarded biography of the Empress Eugénie and afterward to dabble in painting under the tutelage of Whistler. That night he spoke of the little ivory box Marcel had given him when they were lovers. He seized Marcel's hand and kissed it.[37] How little Proust privately thought of Lucien's achievement he probably did not know. A couple of weeks later, Proust reported to Walter Berry that he was spending 850 francs a month on ice cream (usually raspberry) and iced beer, still his only nourishment apart from the occasional stab at a *boeuf vinaigrette.* July, however, seemed to mark a sudden return to health. The nightly hauntings of the Ritz resumed. On July 15 Proust had a rollicking time at the city's new nightspot, Le Boeuf sur le Toit, at 28, rue Boissy-d'Anglas, where Gide and Marc Allégret, Misia Sert, Mistinguett, Diaghilev, and Picasso were among the regular clientele.

Chills and fever had reclaimed him by the end of the month. The July reprieve was over. A letter to Edmond Jaloux accurately reported that he had not left Paris for eight years. Indeed, he would never again leave rue Hamelin. Around July 21, mulling the offer made by collector Jacques Doucet of seven thousand francs for proofs and manuscripts of the *Search*, Proust wrote to the Schiffs: "It isn't very agreeable to think that anyone (if anyone still cares about my books) will be able to study my manuscripts, compare them with the definitive texts, and arrive at suppositions that will always be incorrect about my manner of working and the evolution of my thoughts, etc. All that rather bothers me . . . but I have not yet been able to make up my mind clearly about the matter."[38] Wyndham Lewis arrived to draw his portrait, but Proust found he was too weak to sit for it; afterward he managed a scampish letter of apology in which he claimed to have missed his only chance at posterity.[39]

In the pages of *L'Intransigeant* for August 14 Proust made his final newspaper appearance. Asked to reply to the question "What would you do if you knew the world were about to end?" he wrote: "Life would suddenly seem delightful, if we were threatened with death as you suggest. . . . Ah! If only the cataclysm does not happen this time, we should not fail to visit the new galleries at the Louvre, to throw ourselves at the feet of a certain young lady . . . to set off for India. The cataclysm does not take place, we do none of these things, for we find ourselves back in the swing of normal life again, where negligence dulls desire. . . . We'd do better to remember that we are humans and death may come this evening."[40]

Adding to Proust's misery was a chimney fire in rue Hamelin on August 20 that threw everything into an uproar and filled the apartment with asthma-inducing soot. On September 4 he fell five times from dizziness. A week later Schiff arrived with what he presented as alarming news: Scott Moncrieff's announced title for volume one—*Swann's Way*—meant only *à la manière de Swann* in English. False, of course. *Swann's Way* is a fine and natural translation of *Du côté de chez Swan;* alternatives would be *The Walk by Swann's House* or *Along the Path Leading by Swann's House.* It seems Schiff was making mischief, as he wished to supplant C. K. Scott Moncrieff. (The more one knows of Sydney Schiff, the less one likes him.)

One may conclude from this episode how weak Proust's English was, or had become since the days of translating Ruskin. Provoked by Schiff on false grounds, he wrote thus to Gallimard: "I value my work too much to allow an Englishman to demolish it."[41] He would die, sad to say, imagining that Scott Moncrieff, that inspired translator, had travestied him.

Admittedly more legitimate was Schiff's criticism of *Remembrance of Things Past* as a general title, though it's clear Schiff did not possess sufficient knowledge of Shakespeare to recognize Sonnet 30 ("When to the sessions of sweet silent thought, / I summon up remembrance of things past") as the source. It should be said that Proust disliked the title too. It would be superseded only by the Modern Library edition of 1992, and only recently have people stopped saying *Remembrance of Things Past* and started saying *In Search of Lost Time,* the only acceptable rendering of *À la recherche du temps perdu.*

As it became more difficult to speak, owing to asthma, Marcel increasingly communicated with Céleste by memos written on envelopes or fumigation papers. An example from the last week in September: "There's a lot of draught. Have a little Vichy water warmed up for me, this has lost its sparkle. I was unable to ask you for my potatoes, the horrible tart having made me feel sick. I am freezing. Is it warmer in the kitchen than here? . . . Sorry to ring so much."[42]

In mid-October, despite worsening bronchitis, asthma, and a continual dry cough, Marcel refused any further treatment: No more injections, no more pills or syrups. He seems at this point to have given up on physicians altogether, including his brother, whom he shouted down when transfer to the nearby Piccini clinic was proposed. As Carter writes: "Marcel, son and brother of distinguished doctors, refused all medical treatment, trusting instead to his own and Céleste's remedies"—stewed pears and peaches, lime tea, beans in vinegar, café au lait, bicarbonate of soda.[43] Robert helplessly awaited the onset of pneumonia.

On November 4 came a piece of terrible news that Marcel, in and out of consciousness, was in no condition to receive: After years of morphine and alcohol addiction, Jacques Bizet, his first love, had killed himself with a gunshot to the head. On Friday evening, November 17, Proust claimed to be better and said to Céleste that he thought he could eat a bit of sole. Robert arrived at dinnertime. Marcel decided against the sole. He instructed Céleste to send flowers to Dr. Maurice Bize, the physician he'd so often defied, for his many years of kindness. Now it was only Robert he wanted in attendance; and positively no resumption of treatment. He also asked, on that final evening, that flowers be sent to Léon Daudet in recognition of his recent article on *In Search of Lost Time* in the jingoist paper *Action française*, where Daudet had declared Proust's work a classic for all nations and all time.

Until half past three in the morning, Marcel dictated revisions—draft fragments, not altogether coherent, pertaining to the death of Bergotte—to Céleste, then said he was too tired to continue. The breaking-off point is page 136 of the third typescript of *The Captive:* "They [Bergotte's doctors] stood out among themselves, giving each other a prominent, if gloomy, position in the background. . . . They approached the patient, held endless conferences among themselves, but as to talking to him about his condition . . . no, their professional talk was not meant for the sick. How incredibly rude, said Bergotte. He wanted to know how much time." And farther on: "Then one day it all changed. Everything that had always been prohibited was allowed. 'But for example, might I have some champagne?' 'But absolutely, if you'd like.' It was unbelievable. The labels formerly most forbidden were now ordered, and it was this that lent the despicable note to this unbelievable frivolity of dying."[44]

That night he asked Céleste to stay with him. A little before dawn came the probable rupture of a pulmonary abscess, followed by immediate septicemia. Marcel took a sip of coffee, then told of a hallucination. "Don't switch the light off, Céleste. There's a big fat woman in the room . . . a horrible big fat woman in black. I want to be able to see . . ."[45] Now he began to gather up the papers strewn across his bed. This frightened Céleste, who in Lozère had heard it said that dying men gather up things in that way. About noon, against the patient's firm instructions, Dr. Bize was allowed into the room. He administered an injection of camphorated oil. Retaliating, an enraged Marcel pinched Céleste. It would remain the most painful of her memories.

Robert returned and applied cupping glasses, then ordered oxygen tanks brought in. "Monsieur Proust's eyes never left us. It was dreadful." Here is what follows in Céleste's memoir: "We remained there watching him, and he watching us, for about five minutes. Then, suddenly, Dr. Proust went to his brother and bent down tenderly to close Monsieur Proust's eyes, those eyes that had remained upon us, and still were upon us. I said—'Is he dead?'—'Yes, Céleste, it is finished.' It was four thirty in the afternoon."[46]

All glory to Céleste Albaret—"the one and only Céleste," as Tadié calls her, "alone before history."[47] Reynaldo arrived directly. He would telephone and write to various friends through the night and stay until dawn with the body. In accordance with Marcel's instructions, the Abbé Mugnier came to recite prayers. Léon Daudet visited the body, and Paul Helleu and Dunoyer de Segonzac came to make sketches. Summoned by Cocteau, Man Ray took the famous photo. And Jacques Porel arrived with a ring his late mother, Réjane, had worn in Anatole France's *Le Lys rouge* twenty-three years earlier, and placed it on the dead man's finger. Three days afterward, Valentin Louis Georges Eugène Marcel Proust was laid to rest with his mother and father in the cemetery of Père-Lachaise.

* * *

W. H. Auden famously defined the task of the novelist: to be just among the Just, filthy among the Filthy, too—that is, to encompass us in our zoological identity, coax inner life from hiding, fit outer circumstance, sensuous and particular, to the secret sources barging through. Proust professed to lack imagination, yet no shade of human nature could hide from his implacable art. He wrote that the geniuses who produce the greatest works are not those who "live in the most delicate atmosphere, whose conversation is the most brilliant or culture the most extensive, but those who have the power, ceasing suddenly to live only for themselves, to transform their personality into a sort of mirror"—a mirror that transfigures and makes immortal everything that would otherwise vanish.[48]

In the *Search* an entirely new understanding of life is indeed born, and with it the possibility, for each reader, of a new way of living. This culmination of European literature is also a gospel whose tidings are that nothing is lost that seems to be lost. And that nothing is wasted. Mind and heart secrete the whole of what has happened. Like disregarded books in some illimitable library, memories wait patiently in the dark to be summoned again to consciousness. The buried treasure may be more than recollected, the life of life more than awakened, in the most disenchanted hour of the most ordinary day. Thus it is that Time, the only divinity Proust acknowledged, which makes dust of us, also makes us giants—*des géants plongés dans les années*, as the prodigious last sentence of the *Search* declares: "If I were given long enough to accomplish my work, I should not fail, even if the effect were to make them resemble monsters, to describe men as occupying so considerable a place, compared with the restricted place which is reserved for them in space, a place on the contrary prolonged past measure, for simultaneously, like giants plunged into the years, they touch the distant epochs through which they have lived, between which so many days have come to range themselves—in Time."[49] *Finis operis.* Who can hear enough of those tidings? Who does not dread to lose the least part of such wisdom? "One evening at the Ritz," Camille Wixler recalled, "Monsieur Olivier said to me: 'Camille, Monsieur Proust has just died, you know.' Well, I broke down in front of everybody. How was I going to remember all the things Monsieur Proust had taught me?"[50]

NOTES

Translations of quotations from French sources are my own except as otherwise specified in the bibliography.

Prologue

1. As quoted in Steegmuller, *Cocteau*, 296.

2. *The Captive* and *The Fugitive*, vol. 5, *In Search of Lost Time*, 246.

3. Nabokov, *Lectures on Literature*, 210.

4. *Time Regained*, vol. 6, *In Search of Lost Time*, 315.

5. Moss, *The Magic Lantern of Marcel Proust*, 121.

6. *Sodom and Gomorrah*, vol. 4, *In Search of Lost Time*, 121–22.

7. *The Captive* and *The Fugitive*, 101–2.

8. Bowen, "Notes on Writing a Novel," 252.

9. *In the Shadow of Young Girls in Flower*, vol. 2, *In Search of Lost Time*, 605–6. (trans. slightly modified.)

Chapter One

1. Marx, "The Civil War in France," 652.

2. As quoted in Horne, *The Fall of Paris*, 420.

3. Francis and Gontier, *Marcel Proust et les siens*, 32–33, 38.

4. *Jean Santeuil*, 1956, in the chapter "Parents in Old Age," 723–31.

5. Tadié, *Marcel Proust*, 11.

6. *Jean Santeuil*, 726; *Swann's Way*, vol. 1 of *In Search of Lost Time*, 49.

7. As quoted in White, *Marcel Proust*, 26.

8. Dreyfus, *Marcel Proust à dix-sept ans*, 12–13, as quoted in Carter, *Marcel Proust*, 38.

9. Gregh, *L'Âge d'or*, 82.

10. As quoted in Tadié, *Marcel Proust*, 58–59.

11. As quoted in Carter, *Marcel Proust*, 43.

12. *Swann's Way*, 222–23.

13. *Contre Sainte-Beuve*, ed. Fallois, 55.

14. As quoted in Carter, *Marcel Proust*, 52–53.

15. *Jean Santeuil*, 46.

16. *Selected Letters*, 1: 10–11.

17. Ibid., 1: 24–25.

18. *Correspondance*, 1: 116.

19. Ibid., 21: 550–51.

20. *Hommage à Marcel Proust*, January 1923 issue of *Nouvelle Revue Française*, 146.

21. *Correspondance*, 1: 121.

22. See testimony of Louis Weulersse, Darlu's grandson, in Ferré, *Les années de collège de Marcel Proust*, 249.

23. See Carter, *Marcel Proust*, 93, and *Correspondance*, 21: 157.

24. See Carter, *Marcel Proust*, 94, and his note on 821.

25. *In the Shadow of Young Girls in Flower*, 615.

26. Gregh, *L'Âge d'or*, 183.

27. As quoted in Thurman, *Secrets of the Flesh*, 87.

Chapter Two

1. As quoted in Carter, *Marcel Proust*, 104.
2. *The Guermantes Way*, 168.
3. The final illness and death of Grand'mère are in *The Guermantes Way*, 419–71.
4. Ibid., 80.
5. As quoted in Painter, *Marcel Proust*, 1: 116.
6. Nouvelle Revue Française was the name of both a publishing house and the journal it published. In subsequent text references the journal title will be spelled out and italicized, while the publishing house will be abbreviated as NRF.
7. *Pleasures and Days*, 242–43.
8. *Sodom and Gomorrah*, 21.
9. See Tadié, *Marcel Proust*, 129–37.
10. As quoted in Carter, *Marcel Proust*, 129.
11. *The Guermantes Way*, 69.
12. As quoted in Carter, *Marcel Proust*, 138.
13. As quoted in Tadié, *Marcel Proust*, 202.
14. Ibid., 157.
15. The quotation is from Élisabeth de Clermont-Tonnerre and is in Edgar Munhall, *Whistler and Montesquiou: The Butterfly and the Bat*, Frick Collection (1995), 40–41.
16. *In the Shadow of Young Girls in Flower*, 466.
17. Cocteau, *Le Passé défini*, 1: 293.
18. *Selected Letters*, 1: 50–51.
19. Montesquiou, *Les Pas effacés*, 2: 295.
20. Blanche, *Mes Modèles*, 112.
21. Maurois, *Proust*, 34.
22. Tadié, *Marcel Proust*, 141.
23. *Selected Letters in English*, 1: 57.
24. Carter, *Marcel Proust*, 141.
25. *Pleasures and Days*, 110–11.
26. Tadié, *Marcel Proust*, 202.
27. Cocteau, *Portraits-souvenir*, 188.
28. As quoted in Tadié, *Marcel Proust*, 227.

29. As quoted in Bredin, *The Affair*, 25.

30. As quoted ibid., 7.

Chapter Three

1. *Selected Letters*, 1: 101.

2. *The Captive* and *The Fugitive*, 113–14.

3. As quoted in Tadié, *Marcel Proust*, 214.

4. As quoted in Carter, *Marcel Proust*, 196.

5. *Jean Santeuil*, 374.

6. *Pleasures and Days*, 140.

7. *Contre Sainte-Beuve*, ed. Clarac and Sandre, 5: 399–402.

8. Tadié, *Marcel Proust*, 210.

9. *Jean Santeuil*, 660.

10. *Selected Letters*, 1: 93–94 (trans. slightly modified).

11. *Marcel Proust on Art and Literature*, 325.

12. *Selected Letters*, 1: 105.

13. Ibid., 1: 121.

14. Tadié, *Marcel Proust*, 254.

15. Maurois, *Proust*, 75.

16. "En relisant Marcel Proust," *Nouvelle Revue Française Hommage*, 110.

17. *Lettres à R. Hahn*, 69.

18. *Selected Letters*, 1: 153, and see note 1.

19. Albaret, *Monsieur Proust*, 180–81.

20. See Angelo Rinaldo, "Lulu et les monstres," *L'Express*, December 1, 1991.

21. Correspondance, 13: 389–90.

22. Ibid., 3: 87.

23. *Nouvelle Revue Française Hommage*, 260.

24. Tadié, *Marcel Proust*, 298, and see Michael Levey, *The Case of Walter Pater*, Thames and Hudson, 1978.

25. *Contre Sainte-Beuve*, ed. Clarac and Sandre, 140.

Chapter Four

1. I am particularly indebted in what follows to Louis Begley's definitive analysis and chronology in *Why the Dreyfus Affair Matters*.

2. Blum, *Souvenirs sur l'affaire*, 83, 25.

3. *Jean Santeuil*, 320.

4. *The Captive* and *The Fugitive*, 46.

5. *The Guermantes Way*, 548–49.

6. *Sodom and Gomorrah*, 107–8.

7. *Selected Letters*, 1: 196.

8. *Correspondance*, 14: 337–38.

9. "Rembrandt," in *On Art and Literature*, 336–44.

10. *Time Regained*, 291.

11. A book based on Marie's correspondence with Proust, *The Translation of Memories: Recollections of the Young Proust*, compiled by P. F. Preswich, appeared in 1999.

12. Carter, *Marcel Proust*, 283.

13. *Correspondance*, 2: 377.

14. Ibid., 2: 384.

15. As quoted in Carter, *Marcel Proust*, 636.

Chapter Five

1. *The Captive* and *The Fugitive*, 555–56.

2. *Contre Sainte-Beuve*, 139.

3. *The Captive* and *The Fugitive*, 847.

4. As quoted in Tadié, *Marcel Proust*, 366.

5. *Sodom and Gomorrah*, 465.

6. Tadié, *Marcel Proust*, 360.

7. *Selected Letters*, 1: 196.

8. Tadié, *Marcel Proust*, 321.

9. *Contre Sainte-Beuve*, ed. Clarac and Sandre, 182.

10. *Correspondance* 3: 190.

11. Ibid., 3: 196.

12. *Selected Letters*, 1: 288–91.

13. As quoted in Muhlstein, *Monsieur Proust's Library*, 33.

14. Valentine Thomson, "My Cousin Marcel Proust," *Harper's Magazine*, May 1932, 710–20.

15. *Correspondance*, 3: 363.

16. *Textes retrouvés*, 173–80.

17. *Correspondance*, 3: 418–19.

18. Carter, *Marcel Proust*, 331.
19. *Selected Letters*, 1: 359–60.
20. *Correspondance*, 4: 293.

Chapter Six

1. *Selected Letters*, 2: 33–34.
2. *Swann's Way*, 64.
3. *Selected Letters*, 2: 60.
4. As quoted in the front matter to *Swann's Way*, vi.
5. *On Reading*, 99–129 passim.
6. *Correspondance*, 5: 140.
7. *The Guermantes Way*, 427.
8. *Correspondance*, 5: 345.
9. Ibid., 6: 28.
10. Albaret, *Monsieur Proust*, 169–70.
11. Duplay, *Mon Ami Marcel Proust*, 112.
12. *Correspondance*, 6: 38.
13. *Selected Letters*, 2: 235.
14. Ibid., 2: 230.

Chapter Seven

1. *The Guermantes Way*, 394.
2. *Selected Letters*, 2: 329, and see notes 3, 5.
3. *Contre Sainte-Beuve*, ed. Clarac and Sandre, 5: 67.
4. *Correspondance*, 8: 67.
5. *Selected Letters*, 2: 365–66.
6. *Correspondance*, 8: 139.
7. *Time Regained*, 306.
8. Tadié, *Marcel Proust*, 508.
9. *Correspondance*, 9: 119.
10. Ibid., 8: 93.
11. Ibid., 8: 208.
12. *The Guermantes Way*, 767.
13. See Plantevignes, *Avec Marcel Proust*.
14. *Le Carnet de 1908*, 60–61.

15. Tadié, *Marcel Proust*, 519.
16. *Correspondance*, 8: 320.
17. *Le Carnet de 1908*, 60–61.
18. Tadié, *Marcel Proust*, 520.
19. *Le Carnet de 1908*, 45.
20. *The Captive* and *The Fugitive*, 314–15.
21. The existence of this significant letter was revealed by F. Callu in the *Bulletin de la Bibliothèque Nationale*, March 1980, 12–14.
22. In the Proust archives of the Bibliothèque Nationale, the relevant *cahiers* are numbered 1, 2, 3, 4, 5, 6, 7, 8, 12, 22, 25, 26, 27, 29, 31, 32, 36, 51, 63, and 69.
23. Carter, *Marcel Proust*, 468.

Chapter Eight

1. *Correspondance*, 21: 29.
2. In *L'Intransigeant*, September 21, 1910.
3. Cocteau, *Opium*, 160–61.
4. *Correspondance*, 10: 169.
5. See *Selected Letters*, 2: 45.
6. "Sur *La Chartreuse de Parme*," *Revue Parisienne*, September 25, 1840.
7. *Correspondance*, 10: 217.
8. Ibid., 9: 95.
9. As quoted in Carter, *Proust in Love*, 103.
10. Tadié, *Marcel Proust*, 518.
11. See ibid., 584, and *Correspondance*, 12: 22.
12. *Correspondance*, 11: 286.
13. *Selected Letters*, 3: 97–98.
14. *Correspondance*, 11: 240.
15. See H. Bonnet, *Le Figaro Littéraire*, December 8, 1966, for the identification of Fasquelle's reader.
16. As quoted in Robert, *Comment débuta Marcel Proust*, 9.
17. *Selected Letters*, 3: 158–59.
18. *Correspondance*, 12: 269.
19. Ibid., 13: 28.

20. *Selected Letters*, 3: 168–69.
21. Ibid., 3: 185–86.
22. *Correspondance*, 17: 193–94.
23. *Selected Letters*, 3: 221, and see note 1.

Chapter Nine

1. As quoted in Homans, *Apollo's Angels*, 312.
2. *Swann's Way*, 488.
3. *Selected Letters*, 3: 207.
4. *Correspondance*, 12: 175–76, notes 1, 2.
5. See appendix in Shattuck, *Marcel Proust*, 166–72, for complete text of interview.
6. *Correspondance*, 12: 314.
7. Ibid., 12: 333, and see note 7.
8. Carter, *Marcel Proust*, 558.
9. *Selected Letters*, 3: 225–26.
10. *Correspondance*, 13: 98.
11. *In the Shadow of Young Girls in Flower*, 281.
12. *Selected Letters*, 3: 232–33.
13. Ibid., 3: 235.
14. Ferdinand Collin, *Parmi les précurseurs du ciel* (Peyronnet, 1948), 254–57.
15. *Correspondance*, 13: 217–23.
16. Ibid., 13: 271.
17. Ibid., 13: 283.
18. *Selected Letters*, 3: 29.
19. *Time Regained*, 164.
20. *Correspondance*, 13: 354.
21. Ibid., 14: 213.
22. *Time Regained*, 227.
23. Carter, *Marcel Proust*, 589.
24. *Selected Letters*, 3: 280–82.
25. Carter, *Marcel Proust*, 592.

26. Edith Wharton, *A Backward Glance* (Charles Scribner's Sons), 1934, 324.

Chapter Ten

1. Pierre Assouline, *Gaston Gallimard: Un demi-siècle d'édition française* (Balland, 1984), 78–79.

2. *Time Regained*, 98. *Cahier* 74 at the Bibliothèque Nationale, marked "Babouche," contains Proust's earliest notes for the account of the war in *Time Regained.*

3. Ibid., 106.

4. Ibid., 120–21.

5. Ibid.

6. *Correspondance*, 14: 130.

7. Tadié, *Marcel Proust*, 612.

8. *In the Shadow of Young Girls in Flower*, 281.

9. Proust's post-1914 expansion of the Albertine material is in *cahiers* 46, 53, 55, 56, 72, and 73.

10. *Correspondance*, 14: 281.

11. *Selected Letters*, 3: 330.

12. *Correspondance*, 15: 54.

13. *Time Regained*, 53–54.

14. *The Captive* and *The Fugitive*, 538.

15. Ibid., 114.

16. Ibid., 114–15.

17. *Letters of Marcel Proust*, 434.

18. Arthur Schopenhauer, *The World as Will and Representation*, trans. E. F. Payne (Dover, 1969), 1: 264.

19. *Swann's Way*, 294–308 and passim.

20. Ibid., 337.

21. Ibid., 494.

22. *The Captive* and *The Fugitive*, 342.

23. Ibid., 505.

24. *Correspondance*, 15: 136–37.

25. Albaret, *Monsieur Proust*, 193.

26. Ibid., 197.

27. Murat, "Proust, Marcel, 46 ans, rentier."

28. See Bonnet, *Les Amours et la sexualité de Marcel Proust*, 79–85. Faÿ told his version to André Germain, who in turn published it in *Les Clés de Proust*, 71.

29. *The Captive* and *The Fugitive*, 109.

30. Albaret, *Monsieur Proust*, 196.

31. Tadié, *Marcel Proust*, 674.

32. *The Guermantes Way*, 565.

33. *Correspondance*, 15: 132.

34. Ibid., 15: 344.

Chapter Eleven

1. Mugnier, *Journal*, 309–10; and Ghislain de Diesbach, *L'Abbé Mugnier, le confesseur du Tout-Paris* (Perrin, 2003), 230–31.

2. See Pedroncini, *Les Mutineries de 1917*, passim.

3. *Correspondance*, 16: 196–97.

4. See Mauriac's memoir *Du côté de chez Proust*.

5. *Correspondance*, 17: 281.

6. Ibid., 17: 289.

7. Wixler, "Proust au Ritz."

8. *Correspondance*, 17: 367.

9. Tadié, *Marcel Proust*, 601.

10. *Correspondance*, 18: 105.

11. Ibid., 18: 123, note 4.

12. *Selected Letters*, 3: 232–33.

13. *Time Regained*, 93–94.

Chapter Twelve

1. *Correspondance*, 18: 296.

2. *The Captive* and *The Fugitive*, 440.

3. As quoted in Tadié, *Marcel Proust*, 695–96, for the unexpurgated text.

4. See Rivière, *Nouvelles Études*, 146–56, and, for an account of his role among *Nouvelle Revue Française* critics, Georges Poulet,

La Conscience critique (J. Corti, 1971), 60–64, as well as Tadié, *Marcel Proust*, 708.

5. "À propos du 'style' de Flaubert," *Contre Sainte-Beuve*, ed. Clarac and Sandre, 586.

6. *Correspondance*, 19: 284.

7. Ibid., 19: 455–58.

8. As quoted in Diesbach, *Proust*, 707.

9. *Correspondance*, 19: 514.

10. Ibid., 19: 646–47.

11. Albaret, *Monsieur Proust*, 307.

12. *The Guermantes Way*, 544.

13. Mauriac, *Oeuvres autobiographiques*, 317.

14. As quoted in *Correspondance*, 20: 210, note 5.

15. Tadié, *Marcel Proust*, 738.

16. *Correspondance*, 20: 114.

17. Mauriac, *Oeuvres autobiographiques*, 263.

18. *Correspondance*, 20: 228.

19. André Gide, *Journal*, 1124.

20. *Correspondance*, 20: 251.

21. *The Captive* and *The Fugitive*, 245.

22. *Correspondance*, 20: 380.

23. Ibid., 20: 268–69.

24. Ibid., 20: 444.

25. As quoted in Carter, *Marcel Proust*, 762.

26. For a detailed account of Faÿ, see Janet Malcolm's marvelous book on Stein and Toklas, *Two Lives* (Yale University Press, 2007).

27. *Correspondance*, 20: 27.

28. Ibid., 20: 571.

29. Ibid., 20: 586.

30. Hugo, *Le Regard de la mémoire*, 201.

31. As quoted in Carter, *Marcel Proust*, 737.

32. *Correspondance*, 21: 50.

33. Ibid., 21: 77.

34. Albaret, *Monsieur Proust*, 337. (At the Bibliothèque Nationale, *cahier* 20 contains all four drafts of the final sentence.)

35. *Correspondance*, 21: 206.
36. *Sodom and Gomorrah*, 90.
37. Daudet, *Autour de soixante lettres de Marcel Proust*, 241.
38. *Correspondance*, 21: 372–73.
39. Ibid., 21: 347; 441, note 6.
40. As quoted in Tadié, *Marcel Proust*, 769.
41. *Correspondance*, 21: 476.
42. Ibid., 21: 146. The Carlton Lake Foundation at The Harry Ransom Center possesses seventy-nine such notes. See Lake, *Chers papiers*.
43. Carter, *Marcel Proust*, 801.
44. *À la recherche du temps perdu*, 3: 1667.
45. Albaret, *Monsieur Proust*, 355.
46. Ibid., 359.
47. Tadié, *Marcel Proust*, 776.
48. *In the Shadow of Young Girls in Flower*, 175.
49. *Time Regained*, 531–32.
50. Wixler, "Proust au Ritz," 21.

BIBLIOGRAPHY

Works by Proust

À la recherche du temps perdu, ed. J.-Y. Tadié, Bibliothèque de la Pléiade, 4 vols., 1987–89.

Le Carnet de 1908, ed. P. Kolb, Gallimard, 1976.

Chroniques, Gallimard, 1927.

The Collected Poems: A Dual-Language Edition, ed. Harold Augenbraum, Penguin Classics, 2013.

Contre Sainte-Beuve, ed. Bernard de Fallois, Gallimard, 1954.

Contre Sainte-Beuve, together with *Pastiches et Melanges* and *Essais et Articles*, ed. P. Clarac and Y. Sandre, Bibliothèque de la Pléiade, 1971.

Correspondance, ed. P. Kolb, 21 vols., Plon, 1970–93.

Correspondance avec Daniel Halévy, Fallois, 1992.

Correspondance avec Gaston Gallimard, 1912–1922, ed. P Fouché, Gallimard, 1989.

Correspondance avec Jacques Rivière, 1914–1922, ed. P. Kolb, Gallimard, 1976.

Correspondance avec sa mère, ed. P. Kolb, Plon, 1953.

Écrits de Jeunesse, 1887–1895, ed. A. Borrel, Institut Marcel Proust International, 1991.

L'Indifférent, ed. P. Kolb, 1978.

In Search of Lost Time, trans. C.-K. Scott Moncrieff, T. Kilmartin, and A. Mayor, rev. D. J. Enright, 6 vols., Random House/ Modern Library, 1992.

Jean Santeuil, trans. G. Hopkins, introduction by A. Maurois, Simon and Schuster, 1956.

Jean Santeuil, together with *Pleasures and Days*, ed. P. Clarac and Y. Sandre, Bibliothèque de la Pléiade, 1971.

Letters of Marcel Proust, ed. and trans. M. Curtiss, introduction by A. Gopnik, Helen Marx Books and Books and Co., 2006.

Lettres à Reynaldo Hahn, ed. P. Kolb, 1956.

Lettres à sa voisine, ed. E. Gaudrey and J.-Y. Tadié, Gallimard, 2013.

Lettres inédites, ed. P Kolb, Plon, 1966.

Marcel Proust on Art and Literature, 1896–1919, trans. and ed. S. T. Warner, introduction by T. Kilmartin, Caroll and Graff, 1984.

Matinée chez la princesse de Guermantes, Cahiers du "Temps retrouvé," ed. H. Bonnet and B. Brun, Gallimard, 1982.

Mon Cher Petit: Lettres à Lucien Daudet, preface and annotations by M. Bonduelle, Gallimard, 1991.

On Reading, trans. J. Autret and W. Burford, Macmillan, 1971.

Pleasures and Days, ed. T. Laget, Gallimard, 1993.

Selected Letters, ed. P. Kolb, trans. T. Kilmartin, 4 vols., Harper-Collins, 1983–93.

Sésame et les lys by John Ruskin, with notes and introduction by M. Proust, Mercure de France, 1906.

Textes retrouvés, ed. P. Kolb, Gallimard, 1971.

Other Works

Albaret, Céleste, with Georges Belmont [Georges Pelorson]. *Monsieur Proust*, Robert Laffont, 1973.

Arendt, Hannah. "Anti-Semitism," in *The Origins of Totalitarianism*, Schocken, 1951.

Barthes, Roland. "Une idée de recherche," in *Recherche de Proust*, ed. G. Genette and T. Todorov, Éditions du Seuil, 1980.

Beckett, Samuel. *Proust*, Chatto and Windus, 1931.

Begley, Louis. *Why the Dreyfus Affair Matters*, Yale University Press, 2009.

Billy, Robert de. *Marcel Proust: Lettres et conversations*, Éditions des Portiques, 1930.

Blanche, Jacques-Émile. *Mes modèles*, Stock, 1928.

Bloch-Dano, Évelyne. *Madame Proust: A Biography*, University of Chicago Press, 2007.

Blum, Léon. *Souvenirs sur l'Affaire*, Gallimard, 1935.

Bonnet, Henri. *Les amours et la sexualité de Marcel Proust*, Librairie A.-G. Nizet, 1985.

Bouillaguet, Annick. *Dictionnaire Marcel Proust*, Honoré Champion, Dictionnaires et références collection, dir. Brian G. Rogers, 2004.

Bowen, Elizabeth. "Notes on Writing a Novel," *Collected Impressions*, Knopf, 1950.

Bredin, Jean-Denis. *The Affair: The Case of Alfred Dreyfus*, trans. Jeffrey Mehlman, George Braziller, 1986.

Brown, Frederick. *For the Soul of France: Culture Wars in the Age of Dreyfus*, Knopf, 2010.

Brunet, Étienne. *Le Vocabulaire de Marcel Proust, avec l'Index complet et synoptique de "À la recherche du temps perdu,"* 3 vols. Slatkine-Champion, 1983.

Buisine, Alain. *Proust et ses lettres*, Presses Universitaires de Lille, 1983.

———. *Proust. Samedi 27 novembre 1909*, Jean-Claude Lattès, Une journée particulière collection, 1991.

Carter, William. *Marcel Proust: A Life*, Yale University Press, 2000.

———. *Proust in Love*, Yale University Press, 2006.

Clark, Christopher. *The Sleepwalkers: How Europe Went to War in 1914*, Harper, 2013.

Cocteau, Jean. *Opium*, Stock, 1930.

———. *Portraits-souvenir, 1900–1914*, Grasset, 1935.

———. *Le Passé défini*, Gallimard, 1983.

Compagnon, Antoine. *Proust entre deux siècles*, Le Seuil, 1989.
Curtius, Ernst Robert. *Marcel Proust*, Éditions de la Revue Nouvelle, 1928 (trans. from the German edition).
Daudet, Léon. *Salons et journaux*, Nouvelle librairie nationale, 1917.
———. *Souvenirs et polémiques*, Laffont, 1992.
Daudet, Lucien. *Autour de soixante lettres de Marcel Proust*, Gallimard, 1929.
Davenport-Hines, Richard. *A Night at the Majestic*, Faber and Faber, 2006.
David, André. *Soixante quinze années de jeunesse*, A. Bonne, 1974.
de Diesbach, Ghislain. *Proust*, Perrin, 1991.
Dreyfus, Robert. *Marcel Proust à dix-sept ans*, Simon Kra, 1926.
———. *Souvenirs sur Marcel Proust (accompagnés de lettres inédites)*, Grasset, 1926.
Duchène, Robert. *L'Impossible Marcel Proust*, Laffont, 1994.
Duplay, Maurice. *Mon Ami Marcel Proust*, Gallimard, 1972.
Dyer, Nathalie Mauriac. *Proust inachevé, le dossier Albertine disparue*, Honoré Champion, 2005.
Ecksteins, Modris. *Rites of Spring: The Great War and the Birth of the Modern Age*, Houghton Mifflin, 1989.
Faÿ, Bernard. *Les Précieux*, Perrin, 1966.
Ferré, A. *Les années de collège de Marcel Proust*, Gallimard, 1959.
Finkielkraut, Alain. *L'Avenir d'une negation*, Seuil, 1982.
de Fouquières, André. *Cinquante ans de panache*, P. Horay, 1951.
Francis, Claude, and Fernande Gontier. *Marcel Proust et les siens, suivi des souvenirs de Suzy Mante-Proust*, Plon, 1981.
Furet, François. "Les Juifs et la démocratie française," in L'*Atelier de l'histoire*, Flammarion, 1982.
de Gaulle, Charles. *La France et son armée*, Plon, 1934.
Germain, André. *Les Clés de Proust, suivi de Portraits*, Éditions Sun 1953.
Gide, André. *Journal, 1887–1925*, Gallimard, Bibliothèque de la Pléiade, 1996.
Gilbert, Martin. *The First World War*, Weidenfeld and Nicholson, 1994.

Gregh, Fernand. *L'Âge d'or: Souvenirs d'enfance et de jeunesse*, Grasset, 1947.

———. *Mon amitié avec Marcel Proust: Souvenirs et lettres inédites*, Grasset, 1958.

Hahn, Reynaldo. *Notes: Journal d'un musicien*, Plon, 1933.

Halévy, Daniel. *Pays parisiens*, Grasset, 1932.

Hastings, Max. *Catastrophe 1914: Europe Goes to War*, Knopf, 2013.

Homans, Jennifer. *Apollo's Angels: A History of Ballet*, Random House, 2010.

Horne, Alistair, *The Price of Glory: Verdun 1916*, Macmillan, 1962.

———. *The Fall of Paris: The Siege and the Commune 1870–71*, Mamillan, 1965.

Howard, Michael. *The Franco-Prussian War: The German Invasion of France, 1870–1871*, Macmillan, 1961.

Hugo, Jean. *Le Regard de la mémoire*, Actes Sud, 1983.

Jaloux, Edmond. *Avec Marcel Proust*, La Palatine, 1953.

Karpeles, Eric. *Paintings in Proust: A Visual Companion to "In Search of Lost Time,"* Thames on Hudson, 2008.

Keynes, John Maynard. *The Economic Consequences of the Peace*, Macmillan, 1919.

Kirsch, Adam. "Proust Between *Halachah* and *Aggadah*," in *Rocket and Lightship: Essays on Literature and Ideas*, Norton, 2014.

Kolb, Philip. "Proust et Ruskin," *Cahiers de l'Association internationale des études françaises*, Les Belles Lettres, 1960.

———. "The Making of a Novel," *Marcel Proust, 1871–1922: A Centennial Volume*, ed. Peter Quennell, Simon and Schuster, 1971.

Lake, Carlton. *Chers papiers: Mémoires d'un archéologue littéraire*, Seghers, 1991.

Lauris, Georges de. *Souvenirs d'une belle époque*, Amiot-Dumont, 1948.

Lazare, Bernard. *Une erreur judiciaire*, P.-V. Stock, 1897.

Macksey, Richard. "'Conclusions' et 'Incitations': Proust à la recherche de Ruskin," *Modern Language Notes* 96, no. 5 (December 1981).

Marc-Lipiansky, Mireille. *La naissance du monde proustien dans* Jean Santeuil, Nizet, 1974.

Marrus, Michael. *The Politics of Assimilation: A Study of the French-Jewish Community at the Time of the Dreyfus Affair*, Oxford University Press, 1971.

Marx, Karl. "The Civil War in France," in *The Marx-Engels Reader*, 2nd ed., ed. Robert Tucker, Norton, 1972.

Mauriac, Claude. *Proust*, Seuil, 1953.

Mauriac, François. *Du côté de chez Proust*, La Table Ronde, 1947.

———. "L'Affaire Dreyfus vue par un enfant," preface to *Cinq Années de ma vie* by Alfred Dreyfus, Fasquelle, 1962.

———. *Oeuvres autobiographiques*, Gallimard, 1990.

Maurois, André. *À la recherche de Marcel Proust*, Hachette, 1949.

———. *Le Monde de Marcel Proust*, Hachette, 1960.

———. *Proust: Portrait of a Genius*, trans. G. Hopkins, Carroll and Graf, 1984. [Translation of *À la recherche de Marcel Proust*.]

Mitterand, Henri. *Zola journaliste*, A. Colin, 1962.

Morand, Paul. *Le Visiteur du soir*, La Palatine, 1949.

Moss, Howard. *The Magic Lantern of Marcel Proust*, Macmillan, 1962.

Mugnier, Abbé. *Journal*, Mercure de France, 1985.

Muhlstein, Anka. *Monsieur Proust's Library*, Other Press, 2012.

Murat, Laure. "Proust, Marcel, 46 ans, rentier: Un individu 'aux allures de pederastie' fiche à la police," *La Revue littéraire* 14 (May 2005).

Nabokov, Vladimir. *Lectures on Literature*, Harcourt Brace Jovanovich, 1980.

Naturel, Mireille, and Patricia Mante-Proust. *Marcel Proust: l'arche et la colombe*, Michel Lafon, 2012.

Nemerov, Howard. *The Oak and the Acorn*, Louisiana State University Press, 1987.

Painter, George. *Marcel Proust: A Biography*, 2 vols., Random House, 1959, 1965.

Panzac, Daniel. *Le Docteur Adrien Proust*, L'Harmattan, 2003.

Péchenard, Christian. *Proust à Cabourg*, Quai Voltaire 1992; *Proust et son père*, Quai Voltaire 1993; *Proust et Céleste*, La Table Ronde; published in one volume as *Proust et les autres*, La Table Ronde, 1999.

Pedroncini, Guy. *Les Mutineries de 1917*, Presses Universitaires de France, 1967.
Péguy, Charles. *Notre jeunesse*, Gallimard, 1913.
Pinter, Harold. *The Proust Screenplay*, Grove, 1977.
Piperno, Alessandro. *Proust anitebreo*, FrancoAngeli, 2000.
Plantevignes, Marcel. *Avec Marcel Proust, causeries, souvenirs sur Cabourg et boulevard Haussmann*, A. G. Nizei, 1966.
Poliakov, Léon. *Histoire de l'antisémitisme*, Calmann-Lévy, 1973.
Prestwich, P. F. *The Translation of Memories: Recollections of the Young Proust from the Letters of Marie Nordlinger*, Peter Owen, 1999.
Récanati, Jean. *Profils juifs de Marcel Proust*, Buchet Chastel, 1979.
Reinach, Joseph. *Histoire de l'Affaire Dreyfus*, 6 vols., Fasquelle, 1901–11.
Reinach, Théodore. *Histoire sommaire d l'Affaire Dreyfus*, Ligue des Droits de l'Homme, 1924.
Ried, Piers Paul. *The Dreyfus Affair*, Bloomsbury, 2012.
Rinaldo, Angelo. "Lulu et les monstres," *L'Express*, December 1, 1991.
Rivers, J. E. *Proust and the Art of Love*, Columbia University Press, 1980.
Rivière, Jacques. *Nouvelles Études*, 2nd ed., Gallimard, 1947.
Robb, Graham. *Strangers: Homosexual Love in the Nineteenth Century*, Norton, 2003.
———. *Parisians: An Adventure History of Paris*, Norton, 2010.
Rostand, Maurice. *Confessions d'un demi-siècle*, La Jeune Parque, 1947.
Shattuck, Roger. *The Banquet Years*, Harcourt Brace, 1958.
———. *Marcel Proust*, Princeton University Press, 1974.
———. *Proust's Way: A Field Guide to Proust's "In Search of Lost Time,"* Norton, 2000.
Soupault, Robert. *Proust du côté de la médicine*, Plon, 1967.
Sprinker, Michael. *History and Ideology in Proust: "À la recherche du temps perdu" and the Third French Republic*, Verso, 1998.
Steegmuller, Francis. *Cocteau: A Biography*, Little, Brown, 1970.
Strachan, Hew. *The First World War*, Viking, 2003.
Tadié, Jean-Yves. *Marcel Proust*, trans. Euan Cameron, Viking, 2000.
———. *De Proust à Dumas*, Gallimard, Blanche collection, 2006.
———. *Le Lac Inconnu: Entre Proust et Freud*, NRF/Gallimard, 2012.

Thomson, Valentine. "My Cousin Marcel Proust," *Harper's Magazine* 164 (May 1932).

Thurman, Judith. *Secrets of the Flesh*, Knopf, 1999.

Tuchman, Barbara W. *The Guns of August*, Macmillan, 1962.

———. *The Proud Tower: A Portrait of the World Before the War, 1890–1914*, Macmillan, 1966.

de Waal, Edmund. *The Hare with Amber Eyes: A Family's Century of Art and Loss*, Chatto and Windus, 2010.

Walsh, Stephen. *Stravinsky: A Creative Spring, Russia and France, 1882–1934*, Knopf, 1999.

Weber, Eugen. *Action française*, Stock, 1972.

White, Edmund. *Marcel Proust*, Viking Penguin, 1999.

Wixler, Camille. "Proust au Ritz: souvenirs d'un maître d'hôtel," *Adam International Review* 40, nos. 394–96 (1979).

Yoshikawa, Kazuyoshi, et al. *Indexe Générale de la correspondance de Marcel Proust d'après l'édition de Philip Kolb*, Presses de l'Université de Kyoto, 1998.

ACKNOWLEDGMENTS

All students of Proust are deeply indebted to Philip Kolb, whose twenty-one-volume edition of the correspondence is surely among the greatest scholarly feats of all time. Without the archival depths of Jean-Yves Tadié's biography, I couldn't have made a beginning. Without William C. Carter's exemplary biography in English—never to be bettered for its storytelling vigor—I couldn't have found a way through the maze.

I wish to express my heartfelt gratitude to the John Simon Guggenheim Memorial Foundation, to its president, Edward Hirsch, and to its vice president, André Bernard, for support during the two years I worked on this book; to Professor Nicholas Dames, former chair of Columbia University's Department of English and Comparative Literature, who allowed me to conduct a seminar on Proust in the spring term of 2013; and to the talented students of that cohort, whose insights hastened my own. Joel Conarroe, Richard Howard, Catherine Healey, Patricia O'Toole, and Noel Ice gave generously of their time. Erica Hanson has been my faithful guide at Yale University Press. Patrick Callihan kindly secured the photo permissions. Dan Heaton has been the most scrupulous of copy editors. Wendy Strothman watched over my interests at every stage. Profound thanks are owed to Steven Zipperstein and Anita Shapira, coeditors of the Jewish Lives series, who invited me to write this book; and to Leon Black, whose generosity has made the series possible.

Nothing I say here about Ileene Smith, my incomparable editor, will suffice.

INDEX

Titles are by Proust unless otherwise noted. Photographs are indicated by italicized page numbers.

Jewish Lives is a major series of interpretive biography designed to illuminate the imprint of Jewish figures upon literature, religion, philosophy, politics, cultural and economic life, and the arts and sciences. Subjects are paired with authors to elicit lively, deeply informed books that explore the range and depth of Jewish experience from antiquity through the present.

Jewish Lives is a partnership of Yale University Press and the Leon D. Black Foundation.

Ileene Smith is editorial director. Anita Shapira and Steven J. Zipperstein are series editors.

PUBLISHED TITLES INCLUDE:

Ben-Gurion: Father of Modern Israel, by Anita Shapira
Bernard Berenson: A Life in the Picture Trade, by Rachel Cohen
Sarah: The Life of Sarah Bernhardt, by Robert Gottlieb
Leonard Bernstein: An American Musician, by Allen Shawn
Léon Blum: Prime Minister, Socialist, Zionist, by Pierre Birnbaum
David: The Divided Heart, by David Wolpe
Moshe Dayan: Israel's Controversial Hero, by Mordechai Bar-On
Einstein: His Space and Times, by Steven Gimbel
Becoming Freud: The Making of a Psychoanalyst, by Adam Phillips
Emma Goldman: Revolution as a Way of Life, by Vivian Gornick
Hank Greenberg: The Hero Who Didn't Want to Be One, by Mark Kurlansky
Peggy Guggenheim: The Shock of the Modern, by Francine Prose
Lillian Hellman: An Imperious Life, by Dorothy Gallagher
Jabotinsky: A Life, by Hillel Halkin
Jacob: Unexpected Patriarch, by Yair Zakovitch
Franz Kafka: The Poet of Shame and Guilt, by Saul Friedländer
Rav Kook: Mystic in a Time of Revolution, by Yehudah Mirsky
Primo Levi: The Matter of a Life, by Berel Lang
Moses Mendelssohn: Sage of Modernity, by Shmuel Feiner
Proust: The Search, by Benjamin Taylor
Walter Rathenau: Weimar's Fallen Statesman, by Shulamit Volkov
Mark Rothko: Toward the Light in the Chapel, by Annie Cohen-Solal

Solomon: The Lure of Wisdom, by Steven Weitzman
Leon Trotsky: A Revolutionary's Life, by Joshua Rubenstein

FORTHCOMING TITLES INCLUDE:

Rabbi Akiva, by Barry Holtz
Irving Berlin, by James Kaplan
Hayim Nahman Bialik, by Avner Holtzman
Louis Brandeis, by Jeffrey Rosen
Martin Buber, by Paul Mendes-Flohr
Benjamin Disraeli, by David Cesarani
Bob Dylan, by Ron Rosenbaum
George Gershwin, by Gary Giddins
Allen Ginsberg, by Edward Hirsch
Ben Hecht, by Adina Hoffman
Heinrich Heine, by Fritz Stern
Theodor Herzl, by Derek Penslar
Jesus, by Jack Miles
Groucho Marx, by Lee Siegel
Karl Marx, by Shlomo Avineri
Moses, by Avivah Zornberg
J. Robert Oppenheimer, by David Rieff
Rabin, by Itamar Rabinovich
Jerome Robbins, by Wendy Lesser
Julius Rosenwald, by Hasia Diner
Jonas Salk, by David Margolick
Steven Spielberg, by Molly Haskell
Barbra Streisand, by Neal Gabler
The Warner Brothers, by David Thomson
Ludwig Wittgenstein, by Anthony Gottlieb